4B

Also from EATMS Productions

Books on power, survival, women's autonomy, and the systems shaping modern America.

Nonfiction

Billionaires, Capitalism, and Power

Evil and the Mountain Ungreed
Self Help for American Billionaires
Selfish Steve and the Ivory Tower
Tariffs, Taxes, & Face-Eating Leopards
Ban Billionaires: Fascism Fix

Fascism, Religion, and Cultural Control

Self Help for the Manosphere
Fascism 2025
Fascism & the Perverts & the Greed Virus
Christian Fascism Marriage Book
Tyranny, Table Manners, & Tiramisu

Guides for Women's Autonomy and Protection

How to Survive in Post-America as a Woman
Project 2025 American Drag
4B – Burn, Ban, Boycott, Build
4B OG – So No Go GYN
I'm Glad He's Dead

Analysis of Authoritarian Project 2025

Project 2025: The Blueprint
Project 2025: The List
Project 2025, Christian Dumb Dumbs, & The Republican Agenda
Fascism, Project 2025, & The Pinkprint

Modern Rewrites for Women

Stoic Principles Reimagined
Siddhartha Reimagined
The Prince Reimagined for Women
The Art of War Reimagined for Women
The Jungle Reimagined
The Constitution Reimagined for Women

Machine Learning Series

AI, Bitcoin, Nostr for Women
AI, Safety, & Security for Women
AI, Anxiety, & Health for Women
AI, Kids, & Family Safety for Women
AI, Creativity, & Personal Expression for Women
AI, Independent Work, & Parallel Power for Women

Social Systems Series

Emotional Labor for Women
Household Power for Women
Workplace Power for Women
Medical Bias for Women
Aging Systems for Women
Recovery Systems for Women

Fiction

Dystopian Stories of Resistance and Collapse

Propaganda Paige & the Missing Prosperity
Propaganda Paige & the TIDE Manifesto
Propaganda Paige & the Shadow Cartographers
Propaganda Paige & the Prosperity Alliance
Propaganda Paige & the Shattered Truth
Propaganda Paige & the Rising TIDE
Propaganda Paige & the Last Bastion
Propaganda Paige & the Dawn of Prosperity
Project 2025: Dorian — The Last Men
Project 2025: Boy — A Last Men Novel

4B Movement
BURN
BAN
BOYCOTT
BUILD

F*ck the patriarchy 1

by

Esme Mees

EATMS
PRODUCTIONS

ISBN: 978-1-966014-05-8

Cover, interior design, interior prints by: Esme Mees

eatms@pm.me
www.eatms.me

Printed in the United States of America.

Table of Contents

Prologue:
Enter Post America

AKA Gilead

Here we are. Welcome to Gilead, where the laws are draped in the language of liberty, but the weight of oppression is unmistakable. Population: you. It's a place where your rights are stripped away piece by piece, so slowly and methodically that by the time you notice, you're already shackled. But don't worry, they'll call it "freedom." They'll tell you this is what democracy looks like. They'll remind you that if you just vote a little harder next time, maybe they'll let you have a sliver of what was yours to begin with.

Gilead isn't a future dystopia; it's the reality we live in now. It doesn't come with the blood-soaked drama of rebellion or a tyrant's decree. No, it sneaks in under the guise of protecting the children, preserving family values, saving the soul of the nation. But behind every smiling politician quoting scripture, behind every hand pressed piously to a heart, there's a knife aimed squarely at your autonomy. Your body, your choices, your voice, they're all threats to their precious order, and the more you fight, the more they tighten their grip.

Oh, but they have rules for you, don't they? Be civil. Stay polite. Keep showing up and working within the system. Don't let your anger show, God forbid you scare anyone. Because nothing terrifies the architects of Gilead more than a woman who refuses to play nice. They'll call you hysterical, radical, ungrateful. But here's the thing about gratitude: it's a gift, not a weapon they get to use against you. You owe them nothing.

So, yes, welcome to Gilead. The walls are closing in, the fire is raging, and the world they've built is designed to break you. But here's the thing: this isn't their story anymore. It's yours. This book isn't about how to survive Gilead. It's about how to burn it to the ground.

The History of the 4B Movement

The 4B Movement—Burn, Ban, Boycott, Build—emerged from the ashes of disappointment, exhaustion, and betrayal. Its origins lie in a moment of collective reckoning, when women around the globe realized that the systems they had been told to trust, governments, courts, even social norms, were never designed to serve them. Rights that had been fought for and won, often over decades, were stripped away with stunning speed, leaving women with a bitter question: what was the point of playing by the rules if the rules were rigged?

Inspired by a similar movement in South Korea, where women declared their independence from the "four pillars of heterosexuality" (dating, marriage, sex, and childbirth), the 4B philosophy took root in the West during the early 2020s. Women were witnessing the erosion of reproductive rights, the rise of authoritarian patriarchy, and the normalization of misogyny in public life. Incremental progress had failed. Compromise had failed. Even massive protests had failed to turn the tide. The time for asking nicely was over.

What began as a whisper among feminist thinkers turned into a rallying cry. Women declared their refusal to feed the systems that oppressed them. They would burn the illusions of civility, ban the privileges of those in power, boycott the industries and corporations that sustained inequality, and build new systems rooted in equity and justice. This wasn't just a protest; it was a blueprint for survival and revolution. The movement spread through online platforms, grassroots networks, and global sisterhoods. It was unapologetic, sharp, and deeply practical. The 4B Movement didn't just demand change, it outlined how to achieve it. From disrupting corporate funding pipelines to organizing mutual aid networks, 4B was a call to action that resonated across borders and generations.

Today, the 4B Movement is more than a resistance strategy, it's a declaration of independence. It's a commitment to dismantling what no longer serves us and creating something better in its place. Burn, Ban, Boycott, Build. The fight isn't over, it's just beginning.

Burn: Scorching the Illusions

Burn is the first pillar of the 4B Movement, and it begins with a flame, small at first, but capable of consuming the lies, complacency, and civility that have kept women trapped for centuries. To burn is to dismantle the illusions that have been carefully constructed to keep you obedient and silent. Civility, they tell us, will save us. Compromise, they insist, is the only way forward. Protest, they whisper, but do it politely. These are the myths we've been sold, and it's time to set them ablaze.

Burning isn't about destruction for destruction's sake; it's about clearing the ground for something new. It's the rejection of the false narratives that have been used to justify our oppression. Burn the lie that voting harder is enough when the game is rigged. Burn the idea that your anger is dangerous, it's not; it's necessary. Burn the toxic myth that incremental progress is the best you can hope for. Because guess what? Incremental progress is how we lost our rights in the first place.

This isn't just a metaphor. Burning means taking action. It's about exposing the rot at the heart of the systems that claim to protect us but do the opposite. It's about confronting the hypocrisy of leaders who preach morality while legislating control over your body. It's about refusing to participate in a game where the rules are written to ensure you lose.

Case studies abound movements that have torn down oppressive regimes by first torching the myths that sustain them. Women in Chile burned the symbols of authoritarianism to demand constitutional reform. Iranian women burn their hijabs as acts of defiance against a regime that polices their bodies. Burning is catharsis, yes, but it's also strategy. It's the first step in creating a world where women are no longer chained by the lies they've been told. The fire is already lit. Let it spread. Burn.

Ban: Weaponizing the Tools of Oppression

The second pillar of the 4B Movement, Ban, flips the script on those who have spent centuries wielding power to ban, silence, and control. If they can ban books, ban abortions, and ban your voice from public discourse, why shouldn't we ban their privileges, their platforms, and their unchecked power? Ban is not just a countermeasure; it's a weapon, a calculated, deliberate rejection of the structures and systems that enable oppression.

Banning starts with identifying the sources of power that sustain the patriarchal machine. Tax exemptions for megachurches preaching misogyny? Ban them. Public platforms for hate speech disguised as free speech? Ban them. Corporate subsidies for industries funding anti-woman policies? Ban them. This isn't about fairness; it's about leverage. They've been playing hardball for centuries, it's time we start using their own rules against them.

But Ban isn't just about institutions, it's about narratives. Ban the language that frames oppression as "compromise" or patriarchy as "tradition." Ban the doublespeak that rebrands inequality as "family values." Reclaim the words they've twisted. Freedom is not their exclusive domain. Morality is not synonymous with control. Banning these toxic narratives is as important as targeting their tangible systems of power. This isn't an act of vengeance; it's self-preservation. When someone locks the door to your freedom, you don't wait for them to unlock it. You ban their access to the keys. Women have been told to take the moral high ground, to rise above, to be better. Ban rejects that lie. It's not about being better, it's about winning.

Ban is unapologetic and strategic. It's not reactionary; it's revolutionary. When you remove the tools they use to oppress, you force them to play a different game. A game where the rules are ours, and the stakes are justice. They've banned us long enough. Now it's their turn. Ban them.

Boycott: Stop Feeding the Beast

Boycott is the third pillar of the 4B Movement, a powerful declaration that we will no longer fund or fuel the systems designed to oppress us. It's not a hashtag or a fleeting campaign, it's an economic and cultural rebellion aimed directly at the heart of patriarchy and corporate greed. The engine of oppression runs on your dollars, your labor, your participation. Boycotting means shutting off the fuel supply.

Boycotting isn't symbolic; it's tactical. It's about identifying the corporations, industries, and institutions profiting from the erosion of women's rights and cutting them off. Think of the corporations that donate millions to anti-abortion politicians while marketing their products to women. The media outlets that normalize misogyny under the guise of "balanced reporting." The politicians who take your vote but sell your rights to the highest bidder. By boycotting them, we hit them where it hurts: their bottom line.

But Boycott isn't just about saying no, it's about creating a new economy that reflects our values. Boycott the businesses funding oppression, and redirect your resources to women-led, ethical alternatives. Divest from corporations that exploit, and invest in those building sustainable, equitable futures. Every dollar is a vote, and it's time to start casting them in favor of justice. This isn't a passive protest; it's an act of defiance. It's about starving the beast. The patriarchy relies on your participation to survive. Without your labor, your money, your compliance, it cannot sustain itself. Boycotting sends a message: we will no longer participate in a system that devalues us, exploits us, and robs us of our futures.

History is filled with examples of economic activism bringing giants to their knees, from the Montgomery Bus Boycott to the divestment movement against apartheid. Boycott reminds us that our power isn't just in our voices, it's in our choices. Stop feeding the beast. Starve it, and watch it collapse. Boycott.

Build: Creating a Future That Outlasts Us

Build is the final pillar of the 4B Movement, and it is where the
revolution transforms into a renaissance. Burning, banning, and
boycotting dismantle the oppressive systems that have kept us
shackled, but Build is where we reclaim power, create new systems,
and construct the world we deserve. It is not enough to tear down the
old, we must replace it with something better, stronger, and rooted in
equity, justice, and solidarity.

Building begins with reimagining the very foundations of our society.
For too long, we've been told that the patriarchal system is inevitable,
that there's no alternative to the exploitation of women and the
planet. Build rejects this lie outright. It demands we create spaces
where women thrive, not as an afterthought, but as a priority. We
don't ask for permission to lead; we take the lead.

At its core, Build is about community. It's about creating networks of
mutual aid where women can support each other outside the systems
designed to keep them dependent. It's about building economies that
prioritize fairness over profit, where women-led businesses aren't the
exception but the rule. It's about fostering educational systems that
empower rather than constrain, where girls are taught not just to
succeed within the system but to question and reshape it. Build is also
about resilience. The patriarchy is not going down without a fight,
and we must be prepared to endure. That means building
infrastructure, legal, financial, and social, that can withstand the
inevitable backlash. It means creating art, stories, and cultures that
inspire and sustain us through the struggle. It means building not just
for today, but for tomorrow, ensuring the next generation inherits a
world worth fighting for.

This is not a passive process. Build is radical. It requires action,
imagination, and an unyielding belief in our collective power. We are
not just surviving the systems that tried to break us, we are creating
systems that will sustain us. Build isn't the end of the fight; it's the
beginning of a new future. Build boldly, and build to last.

Why This Isn't Your Grandma's Feminism (But Maybe It
Should Have Been)

This isn't your grandma's feminism. Or maybe it is, depending on
your grandmother. If she was a suffragist throwing rocks through
windows for the right to vote, if she marched with the Women's
Liberation Movement, demanding equal pay and reproductive rights,
then yes, this might feel familiar. But if her feminism was a softer kind,
polite requests for equality, focused on leaning in without toppling
over, then no, this isn't that. This is sharper, louder, and angrier,
because it has to be.

Your grandma's feminism, in all its forms, laid the groundwork. It
pushed boundaries, opened doors, and shattered ceilings. But it also
stopped short, often constrained by the idea that women could only
demand so much, so fast, and so loud. Many feminists of the past
were forced to accept half-measures, partial rights, partial progress,
and the illusion of equality, because they were told that was all they
could get. Be patient, they were told. Play nice. Compromise. And
while they achieved incredible victories, those compromises came at a
cost. The rights they won, the spaces they carved out, were never
secure. They were always conditional, always vulnerable to backlash.

And here we are, living in the backlash. Reproductive rights are
vanishing. The gender pay gap persists. Violence against women
remains a global epidemic. Climate change, a crisis disproportionately
affecting women, is barreling toward catastrophe. For every step
forward, there has been a clawing, snarling step back. Feminism, as it
was practiced by many in the past, didn't anticipate this level of
hostility, this depth of resistance. It didn't prepare us for a world that
would work so hard to undo everything it gave us.

This isn't to say your grandma's feminism was wrong. Far from it. It
was a necessary first step. It was a beacon in a dark time, and we owe
everything to the women who carried it forward, often at great
personal cost. But it was a product of its time, and its time wasn't as
brutal as ours. The threats we face now, the rise of authoritarianism,
the rollback of rights, the weaponization of religion and "family
values" against us, require a different approach. A feminism that
doesn't just ask but takes. One that doesn't settle for incremental
progress but demands structural change. A feminism that doesn't

hesitate to burn down the structures that harm us, even if that makes some people uncomfortable.

Maybe this is where we circle back to your grandma's feminism, the kind that existed before feminism was a buzzword, before it became a T-shirt slogan or a marketing strategy. The feminism of suffragists chaining themselves to fences, of women on strike in the textile mills, of underground abortion networks risking everything to save lives. That kind of feminism wasn't polite, and it certainly wasn't palatable. It was angry, unapologetic, and deeply uncomfortable for the people it targeted. And it worked.

But somewhere along the way, feminism became nicer. It got watered down, packaged for mass consumption. It started asking for equality instead of demanding it, leaning in instead of knocking down. It got comfortable with being liked. And in that comfort, we lost some of our edge. We let civility replace urgency. We let the incremental replace the revolutionary.

Well, no more. This isn't a time for politeness, and it's definitely not a time for incrementalism. This is a time for feminism that scares people, feminism that disrupts, dismantles, and rebuilds. A feminism that doesn't just want a seat at the table but flips the damn table over when it's clear the table was built to exclude us. If that makes some people uncomfortable, good. Change doesn't come from comfort. It comes from discomfort, from anger, from the refusal to accept the world as it is.

And maybe that's what your grandma's feminism was always about. Not the kind written about in history books, sanitized for the sake of heroism, but the kind she lived. The kind that made her late for dinner because she was at a protest. The kind that got her labeled "difficult" because she asked questions no one wanted to answer. The kind that made her burn with a fire that refused to go out, even when the world told her she was asking for too much.

This isn't your grandma's feminism in its compromises or hesitations. But in its anger, its urgency, and its refusal to back down? Oh, it absolutely is. And maybe that's the point. Maybe the feminism we need now isn't new at all. Maybe it's the kind your grandma whispered about when no one else was listening, the kind she dreamed of when she realized the fight wasn't over. Maybe this feminism is hers, finally unleashed, unapologetic, and ready to finish what she started.

Are you really listening now? This is not a joke or a dress rehearsal. Pay attention. What has been tried before has not worked. The solutions now must be different and radical, or else. This isn't a time for waiting, for hoping the pendulum swings back on its own. The stakes are too high, the threats too immediate. These Misogynists are proven liars, we cannot believe them when they say it will be alright. Nor can we believe our so-called liberal allies that are bought and paid for by corporate interests that literally do not care if we live or die. Our conform, our lives is an inconvenience to them.

No. This is a time for all-out, relentless action, feminism that grabs the wheel and wrenches it away from those driving us into oblivion. We are not just fighting for our rights anymore; we are fighting for our lives, for the planet, for the future of everyone who comes after us. The urgency is now, the responsibility is ours, and the cost of failure is unthinkable. We cannot afford to be quiet. We cannot afford to be polite. This is the moment to unleash every ounce of conviction, to carry forward the fire our foremothers lit and set it ablaze across the structures of power that refuse to change.

There is no savior coming to fix this, no cavalry waiting in the wings. We are the saviors, the cavalry, the architects of the revolution. And we will not stop, not until the world reflects the justice and equity that has been denied to us for far too long. This isn't just feminism. This is survival.

A Brief History of How Women's Rights Died, or More Accurately, Were Stabbed, Buried, Dug Up, and Stabbed Again by the Heritage Foundation's Project 2025 and Its Ilk

Women's rights didn't die in a single blow. They were systematically dismantled in a way that would make even the most calculating villains envious. No dramatic fall from grace, no sweeping coup, just a series of insidious, calculated moves. Every rollback was planned, deliberate, and cloaked in the language of morality, family values, and patriotism. And at the helm of this regressive operation was the Heritage Foundation, whose Project 2025 emerged as a blueprint for turning back the clock on decades of hard-won progress.

Let's be clear: the attack on women's rights didn't start with Project 2025, but the playbook they've written took every previous strategy and amplified it to unprecedented levels. Long before this so-called blueprint for a better America was unveiled, the seeds of its ideology had already been planted. The Heritage Foundation has been laying the groundwork for decades, lobbying to reshape the judiciary, crafting anti-woman legislation, and funding campaigns to erode public trust in institutions that dared to advocate for equality.

In many ways, the story begins with Roe v. Wade, a hard-fought victory that enshrined reproductive autonomy as a constitutional right. But even in the years following that decision, the opposition was relentless. Through incremental legislation, restrictive state laws, and an avalanche of lawsuits, they chipped away at abortion access, state by state, clinic by clinic. The Heritage Foundation, along with its allies, fed this campaign, funneling resources to groups like Alliance Defending Freedom and Americans United for Life, ensuring that no corner of the country was untouched by their influence. When Roe was overturned in 2022, it wasn't an isolated event. It was the culmination of decades of meticulous planning, culminating in a Supreme Court shaped by their ideology.

Project 2025 took this momentum and ran with it. Branded as a guide for the next Republican president, the project isn't just a set of policies, it's a roadmap for building a theocratic, patriarchal America. Its proposals range from defunding Planned Parenthood and banning abortion nationwide to rolling back protections for LGBTQ+ people and imposing traditional gender roles under the guise of "protecting the family." The language is Orwellian, but the intentions are clear: to strip women of their autonomy and confine them to roles dictated by a narrow, oppressive interpretation of morality.

One of the most chilling aspects of Project 2025 is its emphasis on reshaping the government itself. It's not enough to pass laws; they want to control the mechanisms that enforce them. From packing federal agencies with ideological loyalists to undermining independent watchdogs, the plan seeks to ensure that even the smallest levers of power are pulled in their favor. The judiciary is a prime example. The Heritage Foundation's fingerprints are all over the nomination process for conservative judges, with a particular focus on those willing to gut women's rights and civil liberties. They understand that lasting change doesn't come from a single presidency, it comes from embedding their values deep within the system.

The irony of their crusade, of course, is that it's wrapped in the language of liberation. The Heritage Foundation and its allies don't frame their efforts as attacks on women; they frame them as defenses of freedom, morality, and tradition. Abortion bans, for instance, are pitched as compassionate efforts to protect unborn lives, never mind the lives of the women who are forced to carry unwanted pregnancies to term. The erosion of workplace protections is framed as empowering women to return to their "natural" roles in the home. It's gaslighting on a national scale, and it's horrifyingly effective.

But perhaps the most insidious element of this campaign is its ability to make the destruction of women's rights seem inevitable. By normalizing their agenda, they've convinced many Americans that this is just the way things are. Rights become privileges, privileges become negotiable, and before you know it, the idea of equality feels like a distant memory. To call this a slow death would be misleading. Women's rights have been stabbed repeatedly, not just by the Heritage Foundation, but by the entire network of think tanks, advocacy groups, and political operatives that share its vision. Each new blow feels like the last, but there's always another waiting in the wings. Stabbed, buried, dug up, and stabbed again, this is the story of how women's rights were not just lost, but violently taken.
The authors of Project 2025 are not merely ideologues scribbling in the margins of American politics, they are the architects of a radical agenda deeply embedded within the next administration, no matter

how vehemently that administration denies involvement. The Heritage Foundation, the think tank behind the blueprint, has long been a pipeline for staffing Republican administrations, crafting policies, and steering judicial appointments. Their fingerprints are everywhere, from judicial nominees to cabinet picks, and their influence is far from benign. The disavowal of any connection to Project 2025 is as hollow as it is calculated, a convenient tactic to distance themselves from its draconian proposals while quietly adopting its core tenets.

Look no further than the alignment between Project 2025's calls for national abortion bans, attacks on LGBTQ+ rights, and the rollback of environmental protections and the rhetoric and actions already taking shape within their orbit. The denials aren't a separation; they're a smokescreen, obscuring a partnership that seeks to redefine democracy into a weapon for minority rule. If we've learned anything, it's this: those who draft these plans know exactly how to infiltrate power, and their denial is simply the first step in making it harder to hold them accountable when the plan is put into motion.

The fight isn't over, but we must understand the scale of what we're up against. This isn't just a battle for policy; it's a battle for the soul of a nation. Project 2025 and its ilk want to erase decades of progress, and they won't stop unless we stop them first. This is a fight for survival, for autonomy, and for the future. And if they think we'll go quietly, they've underestimated us once again.

We Didn't Start the Fire, but We're Damn Sure Not Letting It
Burn Us Alive Without Taking Them Down With Us

We didn't start the fire. That much is certain. The flames of greed,
corruption, and oppression were set long before us, ignited by
centuries of exploitation and fanned by the relentless pursuit of power.
This fire, fueled by inequality, patriarchy, and unbridled capitalism,
has been raging for so long that many have come to see it as
inevitable, a force of nature rather than the product of deliberate,
calculated choices. But just because we didn't start the fire doesn't
mean we'll let it consume us without a fight. This is our mission: to
survive the flames, to extinguish their source, and to rebuild from the
ashes. And if we go down, we're damn sure taking the arsonists with
us.

This fire has taken many forms, economic systems rigged to benefit
the wealthy, laws designed to strip away rights, and a society that
values profit over people. It's the fire of complacency that convinces
us change is impossible, the fire of fear that keeps us silent, and the
fire of complicity that lets injustice thrive. But we are not here to burn
quietly. We are here to resist, to fight back with everything we have.
The flames may be hot, but so is our anger, and anger, when focused,
becomes fuel for revolution. This is not about vengeance; it's about
survival. It's about refusing to be collateral damage in a system
designed to destroy us.

We know what we're up against. The architects of this fire have
names, faces, and fortunes. They wield their power shamelessly,
profiting from our suffering and pretending their greed is virtue. But
their time is running out. We are no longer content to wait for
change, to ask nicely, or to play by their rules. This is a mission of
defiance, of resilience, and of unyielding hope. We didn't start this
fire, but we will damn well put it out. And when we do, we'll ensure it
can never be lit again. This is our promise: to fight, to endure, and to
win, not just for ourselves, but for everyone who comes after us.

Chapter 1~ BURN
Why Burn a Rotten System: Rise of Reeks

The rise of Reek 1 and Reek 2 wasn't just another political shift; it was the apex of a long-brewing storm. Their ascension wasn't born of charisma or coincidence but from decades of deliberate scheming by ideological puppet masters. Organizations like the Heritage Foundation, with their deep pockets and deeper contempt for progress, spent years cultivating the perfect storm of fear, disinformation, and resentment. They didn't just support Reek 1 and Reek 2, they created them. They built their platforms, funded their campaigns, and armed them with a vision: Project 2025. This blueprint, an unflinching guide to authoritarian rule, promised to dismantle the democratic values they claimed to defend while restoring a mythic, hierarchical past that existed only in their imaginations.

Reek 1's rise was not the result of merit or leadership but a grim reflection of a fractured system. He was not a statesman but a spectacle, a bombastic figure who fed on division, leveraging his brashness into a weapon against the very institutions he vowed to protect. He spoke to the disillusioned and disenfranchised, convincing them that their struggles were the fault of "others" rather than the systemic inequalities he would later exploit. Reek 2, his quieter, pious accomplice, served as the perfect counterweight, lending a veneer of religious respectability to their regime's darker ambitions. Together, they created a potent cocktail of fear, resentment, and misguided hope, weaponizing faith and patriotism to consolidate power.

Their weapon of choice? A manufactured crisis. By exploiting long-standing cultural divides, Reek 1 and Reek 2 positioned themselves as the saviors of an America allegedly on the brink of moral and social collapse. The narrative was simple: immigrants were overrunning borders, progressives were dismantling traditions, and secularism was destroying the moral fabric of society. These claims weren't just false; they were deliberate distractions from the real issues plaguing the country, wealth inequality, systemic racism, climate catastrophe, all of which their policies exacerbated. But fear is a powerful motivator, and Reek 1 and Reek 2 wielded it masterfully.

At the heart of their strategy was Project 2025, a document so audacious and authoritarian that its very existence might have been dismissed as paranoia in another era. But in the age of Reek 1 and Reek 2, it became the playbook for a regime bent on dismantling democracy piece by piece. It wasn't just a vision for the future; it was a direct attack on the present. The document outlined plans to undo reproductive rights, gut public education, eliminate LGBTQ+ protections, and cement religious dogma as the law of the land. All of this was couched in the language of patriotism, family values, and God's will, a rhetorical trifecta designed to disarm critics and galvanize supporters.

Reproductive rights were among the first targets. Decades of incremental attacks on abortion access had already eroded the protections enshrined in Roe v. Wade, but Project 2025 aimed to finish the job. Under their regime, abortion was not merely restricted; it was criminalized. Access to contraception was rolled back under the guise of "religious freedom," leaving millions of women without basic healthcare. Reek 2, in particular, championed these measures, cloaking them in the rhetoric of sanctity and divine purpose. But the true purpose was control. By stripping women of their autonomy, Reek 1 and Reek 2 reinforced the patriarchal structures that had long dominated American society, ensuring that women's lives and choices remained subordinate to the state's authority.

The attack on education was no less insidious. Public schools, long a battleground for cultural debates, became a central focus of their war on progress. Project 2025 envisioned a system where history was rewritten, science was sidelined, and critical thinking was all but erased. Discussions of systemic racism, gender identity, and LGBTQ+ rights were labeled as "woke indoctrination" and banned outright. Instead, schools were tasked with instilling patriotism and traditional values, producing a generation of students incapable of questioning the structures that oppressed them. Teachers who resisted were silenced or fired, and parents who protested were painted as radicals. The result was a chilling atmosphere of conformity, where education became a tool of oppression rather than liberation.

And then there was their assault on LGBTQ+ rights. Under the guise of protecting religious freedom, Reek 1 and Reek 2 pushed policies that erased LGBTQ+ identities from public life. Trans individuals were denied healthcare, marriage equality was threatened, and discrimination was not only tolerated but encouraged. This wasn't just policy; it was cultural erasure. By marginalizing LGBTQ+ communities, they sent a clear message: conform or disappear. And for those who refused to disappear? Violence, ostracism, and systemic discrimination awaited, all sanctioned by a state that claimed to be acting in God's name.

While these policies wreaked havoc on marginalized communities, the broader goal was always power. Reek 1 and Reek 2 understood that control required more than just policy, it required reshaping the very fabric of society. They exploited every lever of government, from the judiciary to local school boards, stacking them with loyalists who shared their vision. The Supreme Court, now dominated by ideologues handpicked for their allegiance, became a rubber stamp for their agenda. State legislatures, emboldened by the federal regime, passed draconian laws that mirrored the goals of Project 2025. And through it all, Reek 1 and Reek 2 maintained their grip on power by stoking the flames of division, ensuring that any opposition was fragmented and distracted.

Their use of religion as a weapon cannot be overstated. For Reek 2, faith was both a shield and a sword, wielded to justify policies that harmed the very people his religion claimed to protect. His sermons on morality and sanctity masked the cruelty of his administration's actions, from separating families at the border to cutting social programs that supported the most vulnerable. For Reek 1, religion was less a personal conviction than a convenient tool, a way to manipulate a base eager for a leader who claimed divine favor. Together, they created a theocratic narrative that painted their critics as enemies of God and framed their agenda as a holy mission.

The media landscape only amplified their power. In an age of disinformation, Reek 1 and Reek 2 thrived. Their allies in the media parroted their talking points, vilified their opponents, and distracted the public with manufactured scandals. Social media platforms, despite occasional gestures toward moderation, became breeding grounds for conspiracy theories and hate speech, further polarizing the nation. Meanwhile, independent journalism was under siege, labeled as fake news and undermined by coordinated attacks on its credibility. In this environment, truth became a casualty, and Reek 1 and Reek 2's narrative reigned supreme.

But the consequences of their reign extended far beyond politics. Their policies exacerbated systemic inequalities, leaving millions struggling to survive in an increasingly hostile world. Climate change, ignored and even denied by their administration, wreaked havoc on vulnerable communities. Economic inequality soared as tax cuts for the wealthy gutted social programs and public infrastructure. And the nation's global standing plummeted as alliances were abandoned, human rights abuses were ignored, and authoritarian regimes were embraced.

The rot they introduced was systemic, infecting every level of government and society. It was a deliberate dismantling of the progress made over decades, a rejection of the ideals of equality and justice that had long been the nation's guiding principles. And yet, Reek 1 and Reek 2 framed their actions as a restoration of greatness, a return to a mythical past where America was allegedly at its best. But this vision of greatness was a lie, a fabrication designed to justify oppression and consolidate power.

As their regime tightened its grip, resistance grew. Activists, journalists, and ordinary citizens fought back, exposing the lies and organizing against the policies that threatened their lives and freedoms. But the fight was far from easy. The tools of democracy, free elections, an independent judiciary, a free press, had been weaponized against them, and the stakes had never been higher. Reek 1 and Reek 2 may have risen to power through fear and division, but their reign had ignited a new determination among those who refused to accept their vision for America.

The resistance to Reek 1 and Reek 2 didn't spring forth overnight. It was forged in the crucible of necessity, born out of the realization that the tools of democracy had been turned against the people they were meant to protect. Activists, journalists, educators, and ordinary citizens found themselves at the front lines of a battle not just for policy but for the soul of the nation. The stakes couldn't have been higher. This wasn't just about stopping Reek 1 and Reek 2's theocratic agenda; it was about ensuring that the concept of equality didn't become a relic of history.

Resistance began in the courts, where challenges to their policies flooded the judicial system. But with the Supreme Court and lower courts stacked with loyalists, victories were rare. Nevertheless, these legal battles served as a rallying cry, exposing the cruelty and hypocrisy of their administration and galvanizing public opposition. Grassroots organizing became a powerful force, with activists using every tool at their disposal to mobilize voters, pressure lawmakers, and hold the regime accountable. Social media, often a breeding ground for disinformation, also became a weapon for the resistance, amplifying voices that might otherwise have been silenced.

One of the most striking aspects of the resistance was its diversity. Women, people of color, LGBTQ+ individuals, and immigrants, all groups targeted by Reek 1 and Reek 2's agenda, led the charge. Their lived experiences lent urgency and authenticity to the movement, transforming abstract political debates into deeply personal stories of survival and defiance. These leaders refused to be erased, using their platforms to expose the human cost of the regime's policies and to build coalitions that crossed lines of race, gender, and class.

Artists and writers also played a crucial role, wielding their creativity as a form of rebellion. In the face of censorship and propaganda, they created works that challenged the regime's narrative, preserving the truth in ways that resonated deeply with the public. From satirical sketches that mocked the absurdity of Reek 1's bombast to poignant essays that laid bare the pain of living under their policies, art became a lifeline for those seeking to resist. It reminded people of what was at stake and inspired them to keep fighting.

Despite these efforts, the cultural toll of their reign was immense. Project 2025 wasn't just about dismantling policies, it was about reshaping the very fabric of American identity. By controlling education, media, and public discourse, Reek 1 and Reek 2 sought to erase the progress made by marginalized groups and replace it with a narrative that centered white, Christian, patriarchal dominance. This wasn't just about politics; it was about erasing entire communities from the story of America.

For women, the impact was particularly devastating. Stripped of reproductive autonomy, many found themselves forced into life-altering decisions by a state that cared more about controlling their bodies than supporting their lives. The rollback of workplace protections and social safety nets made it even harder for women to survive, let alone thrive. And yet, women remained at the forefront of the resistance, organizing protests, running for office, and building networks of mutual aid to support those left behind by the system. The LGBTQ+ community faced similar erasure. Anti-trans legislation, "Don't Say Gay" laws, and the normalization of hate speech created a climate of fear and violence.

But like women, LGBTQ+ individuals refused to disappear. They fought back with courage and creativity, building safe spaces, amplifying their voices, and challenging the regime's attempts to legislate them out of existence. Their defiance was a reminder that even in the darkest times, the human spirit cannot be extinguished. The broader public, too, began to wake up to the realities of Reek 1 and Reek 2's America. While many had been seduced by their rhetoric of greatness, the lived experience of their policies was impossible to ignore. Economic inequality soared, climate disasters worsened, and the erosion of civil liberties became an everyday reality. For some, it was too late, they had already lost loved ones to policies that prioritized ideology over humanity. But for others, these failures became a catalyst for action.

The path forward was anything but clear. The institutions of democracy had been weakened, the judiciary was compromised, and the media landscape was dominated by disinformation. But resistance movements found strength in community, using their collective power to push for change. They fought for voting rights, demanding an end to gerrymandering and voter suppression. They supported candidates who shared their vision of equality and justice, refusing to let cynicism or despair dictate their actions.

One of the most critical fronts in this battle was education. Recognizing the long-term consequences of Project 2025's indoctrination agenda, activists and educators worked tirelessly to counter its effects. They developed alternative curricula, created spaces for critical dialogue, and fought to protect academic freedom. It was a slow and grueling process, but it was essential to ensuring that the next generation would not inherit a society defined by ignorance and fear.

Reclaiming the narrative was another vital strategy. Reek 1 and Reek 2 had built their regime on a foundation of lies, using propaganda to manipulate public perception and silence dissent. Countering this required a relentless commitment to truth, whether through investigative journalism, grassroots storytelling, or public art. By exposing the regime's corruption and amplifying the voices of those it sought to silence, the resistance began to chip away at their facade of legitimacy.

But the fight was far from over. Reek 1 and Reek 2's power was deeply entrenched, and their base remained fervent. For many, their promises of a return to a mythic past were still deeply appealing, even as the consequences of their policies became impossible to ignore. The resistance faced an uphill battle, not just against the regime but against the forces of apathy and complicity that had allowed it to rise in the first place.

Yet, even in the face of overwhelming odds, there was hope. The resistance was growing, not just in numbers but in strength and determination. It was learning from the past, adapting its strategies, and building the infrastructure needed to sustain a long-term fight. And most importantly, it was rooted in a vision of the future that rejected the hierarchy and oppression of Reek 1 and Reek 2's America.

That vision was one of true equality, where diversity was celebrated rather than erased, where power was shared rather than hoarded, and where freedom was not a privilege but a right. It was a vision that recognized the humanity of every individual and sought to create a society where that humanity could flourish. And while the road to that future was long and fraught with challenges, the resistance was determined to walk it, together.

Because ultimately, Reek 1 and Reek 2's reign wasn't just a battle for the present; it was a battle for the future. And for all their power and cruelty, they underestimated one thing: the resilience of those who refused to be silenced. The resistance was not just fighting against their vision of America, it was building a new one. And that vision, forged in the fires of defiance and hope, would outlast them all.

Chapter 2~ BURN
Holy Hypocrisy

The moral rot of far-right Christian nationalism is a phenomenon so glaring, so blatantly contradictory, that it almost defies comprehension. Yet, it thrives, unchecked, in a society trained to associate religion with righteousness and patriotism with piety. The movement, which marries a selective interpretation of scripture with the basest instincts of power and control, has positioned itself as a guiding force in American politics. But beneath the surface lies a cesspool of hypocrisy, where the rhetoric of morality masks an insidious agenda and the banner of "Christian values" becomes a license for greed, oppression, and authoritarian rule.

At its core, far-right Christian nationalism is not about faith, it's about power. It's a weaponized version of religion, stripped of humility, compassion, and justice, and reshaped into a tool for enforcing a hierarchical worldview. In this vision, God's kingdom is less a place of love and more a fortress of exclusion, where the privileged reign supreme and everyone else is either subjugated or cast out. The movement claims to be restoring America's moral compass, but in reality, it's dragging the nation into a dystopian landscape where cruelty is policy, hypocrisy is virtue, and scripture is weaponized to justify the indefensible.

Take the pastors with private jets, for example, a grotesque symbol of the greed and excess that permeates this brand of Christianity. These so-called spiritual leaders preach humility and sacrifice to their congregations while living lives of unfathomable luxury. Their mega-churches, with their concert-style services and ATMs in the lobbies, are less houses of worship and more tax-exempt empires. They jet around the world in planes purchased with donations from working-class believers who are told their sacrifices will bring them closer to God. Meanwhile, the pastors live as kings, their opulence a stark contrast to the suffering of their flock. They preach the prosperity gospel, a heretical doctrine that equates wealth with divine favor, convincing the faithful that their struggles are a test of faith rather than a consequence of systemic inequities perpetuated by the very politicians these pastors endorse.

And then there are the politicians themselves, those sanctimonious figures who quote scripture as they strip away human dignity. They stand at podiums, invoking the name of God while passing laws that harm the most vulnerable among us. They claim to be "pro-life," yet their policies betray a callous disregard for life once it leaves the womb. Healthcare? They oppose it. Childcare? Not their problem. Gun control? An infringement on their twisted interpretation of freedom. Their version of pro-life is, at best, pro-birth, an ideology that prioritizes control over compassion, ensuring that women are forced to carry pregnancies to term regardless of their circumstances, only to be abandoned by a society that refuses to support them or their children.

This lie of pro-life is one of the most glaring hypocrisies of far-right Christian nationalism. If they truly cared about life, they would address the systemic issues that threaten it at every turn. They would advocate for universal healthcare, ensuring that no one dies because they can't afford to see a doctor. They would invest in childcare and education, creating a society where every child has the opportunity to thrive. They would support common-sense gun control measures to prevent the epidemic of mass shootings that has turned schools, churches, and shopping malls into killing fields. But instead, they focus their energy on controlling women's bodies, policing queer identities, and enforcing a moral code that prioritizes power over people.

The hypocrisy extends to their economic policies, which betray a flagrant disregard for the teachings of the very scripture they claim to uphold. Jesus spoke of feeding the hungry, clothing the naked, and caring for the sick, yet these politicians champion policies that exacerbate poverty, strip away social safety nets, and funnel wealth to the already wealthy. They oppose raising the minimum wage, dismissing it as socialism, while cutting taxes for corporations and the ultra-rich. They demonize the poor, framing poverty as a moral failing rather than the result of systemic inequality. In their America, the rich are celebrated, the poor are vilified, and the teachings of Christ are conveniently ignored.

And let's not forget their approach to immigration, a glaring contradiction to the biblical call to welcome the stranger and love thy neighbor. They build walls, both literal and metaphorical, to keep out those who seek refuge from violence, poverty, and persecution. They separate families at the border, detaining children in inhumane conditions while claiming to uphold family values. Their rhetoric dehumanizes immigrants, painting them as threats rather than fellow human beings deserving of dignity and compassion. They quote scripture to justify their actions, twisting the words of a faith rooted in love and justice into a justification for hate and exclusion.

The cultural war they wage isn't about morality, it's about control. They decry the decline of traditional values, framing progress as a threat to their vision of America. They target LGBTQ+ individuals, women, and people of color, casting them as villains in a narrative designed to consolidate power in the hands of white, Christian men. They rail against "woke ideology," a term they wield as a cudgel against any movement that challenges their hegemony. They claim to be defending freedom, but their actions reveal a commitment to domination, not liberation.

What makes this hypocrisy even more egregious is its effectiveness. For many, the rhetoric of far-right Christian nationalism is persuasive, offering a sense of certainty in an uncertain world. It provides a scapegoat for societal problems, redirecting anger away from the systems of oppression and toward marginalized communities. It wraps its message in the comforting language of faith and tradition, obscuring the cruelty at its core. And it exploits the very real struggles of its followers, offering them the false promise of empowerment while stripping away their agency and autonomy.

This manipulation is particularly evident in their approach to gender. Far-right Christian nationalism upholds a rigid hierarchy in which men are the leaders and women are the subservient caretakers. This vision is enforced through policies that restrict reproductive rights, undermine workplace protections, and perpetuate gender-based violence. Women are told their worth lies in their ability to bear children and support their husbands, while their ambitions and autonomy are dismissed as threats to the natural order. This isn't just a political stance, it's a deliberate effort to maintain patriarchal control, ensuring that women remain second-class citizens in a society that values power over equality.

Yet, for all its success, the hypocrisy of far-right Christian nationalism is also its greatest vulnerability. The cracks in its facade are becoming harder to ignore. The greed of its leaders, the cruelty of its policies, and the contradictions of its rhetoric are sparking a growing backlash. Activists, faith leaders, and ordinary citizens are speaking out, challenging the narrative that conflates Christianity with oppression. They are reclaiming their faith, emphasizing the teachings of love, justice, and inclusion that stand in stark contrast to the movement's agenda.

The hypocrisy of far-right Christian nationalism may be its greatest vulnerability, but exposing it is no small task. For decades, the movement has entrenched itself in the cultural and political landscape, wrapping its message in the language of faith and patriotism to disarm critics and silence dissent. But as the cracks in its facade grow, so too does the resistance. Across the nation, a diverse coalition of activists, faith leaders, and ordinary citizens is rising up to challenge the lies and reclaim the values of justice, equality, and compassion that the movement has co-opted.

One of the most powerful tools in this fight has been the truth. Far-right Christian nationalism thrives on disinformation, creating an alternate reality where its leaders are righteous saviors and its policies are divine mandates. Countering this requires a relentless commitment to exposing the facts, whether through investigative journalism, public education campaigns, or grassroots storytelling. Activists have worked tirelessly to document the harm caused by the movement's policies, from the devastation of abortion bans to the trauma inflicted on LGBTQ+ individuals by discriminatory laws. These stories, rooted in lived experience, cut through the noise of propaganda and remind people of the real human cost of far-right Christian nationalism.

Faith leaders have also played a crucial role in this resistance, challenging the narrative that Christianity and far-right politics are synonymous. For too long, the movement has claimed to speak for all Christians, using its distorted interpretation of scripture to justify its agenda. But many people of faith reject this vision, emphasizing the teachings of love, inclusion, and social justice that stand in stark contrast to the movement's rhetoric. These leaders are reclaiming their faith, using their platforms to call out hypocrisy and advocate for policies that reflect the true values of their beliefs. From progressive pastors to interfaith coalitions, they are challenging the idea that religion belongs to the far-right and reminding the world that faith can be a force for liberation rather than oppression.

Grassroots organizing has been another cornerstone of the resistance. While far-right Christian nationalism wields immense power at the national level, its influence is often most deeply felt in local communities. From school boards to city councils, the movement has worked to infiltrate every level of government, ensuring that its agenda is enforced in every corner of society. But activists are fighting back, mobilizing voters, running for office, and building networks of mutual aid to counter the movement's influence. These efforts are not just about stopping harmful policies, they are about creating a vision of governance that prioritizes equity and accountability.

One of the most significant battlegrounds in this fight has been reproductive rights. The lie of "pro-life" has been exposed time and again by the movement's refusal to support policies that actually sustain life. Activists have worked tirelessly to highlight this hypocrisy, pointing out the absurdity of a movement that claims to protect life while opposing healthcare, childcare, and gun control. They have documented the devastating consequences of abortion bans, from women forced to carry nonviable pregnancies to term to those who have died because they were denied life-saving care. These stories have galvanized public support for reproductive freedom, sparking protests, legal challenges, and advocacy campaigns that continue to fight for bodily autonomy.

The LGBTQ+ community has also been at the forefront of the resistance, countering the erasure and dehumanization perpetuated by far-right Christian nationalism. Activists have fought back against anti-trans legislation, conversion therapy, and other forms of discrimination, using everything from legal challenges to public demonstrations to amplify their voices. They have created safe spaces and support networks for those targeted by the movement, building resilience and solidarity in the face of hate. Through art, storytelling, and advocacy, they have refused to be silenced, reminding the world that their existence is not up for debate.

Education remains a critical front in this battle. Far-right Christian nationalism's assault on schools is not just about banning books or censoring curricula, it is about controlling the next generation. By erasing discussions of systemic racism, gender identity, and historical injustice, the movement seeks to create a population that is easier to manipulate and control. But educators and activists are pushing back, developing alternative resources, organizing teach-ins, and fighting to protect academic freedom. They are challenging the narrative that education should be a tool of indoctrination, emphasizing the importance of critical thinking, empathy, and truth in creating a just society.

The resistance has also found allies in unexpected places. Artists, musicians, and writers have used their platforms to challenge the movement's narrative and inspire change. From satirical comedy that exposes the absurdity of far-right rhetoric to poignant films and novels that explore the human cost of its policies, art has become a powerful tool for resistance. It not only exposes the hypocrisy of far-right Christian nationalism but also offers a vision of what the world could be, a vision rooted in justice, compassion, and equality.

Economic justice has emerged as another key focus of the resistance, highlighting the ways in which far-right Christian nationalism exacerbates inequality. Activists have called attention to the movement's economic policies, which prioritize tax cuts for the wealthy and corporations while gutting social programs that support working families. They have emphasized the connection between economic insecurity and the rise of authoritarianism, arguing that true justice requires addressing the systemic inequities that leave so many people struggling to survive. By advocating for living wages, affordable housing, and universal healthcare, the resistance is challenging the idea that inequality is inevitable and offering a vision of an economy that works for everyone.

Despite these efforts, the fight is far from over. The movement's power is deeply entrenched, and its leaders are relentless in their pursuit of control. They continue to exploit fear and division, using disinformation and propaganda to maintain their base of support. They wield religion as a weapon, twisting scripture to justify their actions and silence dissent. And they use the tools of government to entrench their power, from gerrymandering and voter suppression to judicial appointments and executive orders.

But even in the face of these challenges, the resistance is growing. It is learning from history, adapting its strategies, and building coalitions that transcend traditional divides. It recognizes that this fight is not just about defeating far-right Christian nationalism, it is about creating a society that values justice, equality, and human dignity. And while the road ahead is long, the resistance remains committed to walking it, driven by the belief that a better world is possible.

The hypocrisy of far-right Christian nationalism is staggering, but its unraveling is inevitable. The movement's contradictions, its claim to be pro-life while opposing policies that sustain life, its invocation of freedom while enforcing oppression, its rhetoric of morality while embracing greed and cruelty, cannot withstand the scrutiny of a people determined to fight for justice. The resistance is not just exposing these contradictions; it is building a vision of the future that rejects them entirely. It is a vision rooted in the belief that every person deserves dignity, every voice deserves to be heard, and every life deserves to be valued.

As the resistance grows, so too does the hope for a future free from the moral rot of far-right Christian nationalism. This is not just a battle for policy, it is a battle for the soul of a nation. And while the forces of oppression are formidable, they cannot overcome the resilience, creativity, and determination of those who refuse to accept their vision for America. The fight continues, but so does the hope. And in that hope lies the promise of a better tomorrow.

The age of polite protests is over. For too long, the fight for justice has been hampered by an obsession with civility, by the misguided belief that change can be achieved by asking nicely and waiting patiently. But history is clear: those who hold power rarely surrender it willingly. Change doesn't come from politeness; it comes from pressure, disruption, and, when necessary, the complete dismantling of systems that refuse to evolve. The 4B Movement—Burn, Ban, Boycott, Build—starts with the recognition that illusions of civility and bipartisan compromise are not bridges to progress but barriers to it. To create real, lasting change, we must set fire to the lies that have kept us compliant and complicit for so long.

The idea that civility alone can transform oppressive systems is one of the greatest illusions of our time. We are told to march quietly, to appeal to the better angels of those in power, to wait for incremental progress. But the truth is, civility has always been a tool of control, a way to ensure that resistance remains manageable and non-threatening. It's no coincidence that calls for civility are often directed at the marginalized, not the oppressors. Civility is wielded as a weapon to silence dissent, to make injustice palatable, and to keep those who suffer under the system from making the powerful uncomfortable. But discomfort is exactly what's needed. Real change doesn't come from polite requests; it comes from disrupting the status quo, from forcing those in power to confront the consequences of their actions.

History is rife with examples of movements that succeeded not through civility but through disruption. The labor strikes of the early 20th century were not polite affairs; they were bold, unapologetic demands for better wages and working conditions, often met with violent resistance. The Civil Rights Movement of the 1960s is often sanitized in history books, its leaders portrayed as paragons of politeness, but the reality is far more complex. The Freedom Rides, sit-ins, and marches were acts of defiance that disrupted public life and exposed the brutality of segregation. Even the American

Revolution, so often romanticized as a noble quest for freedom, was anything but polite. It was a fight, and it was messy.

One of the clearest case studies in the necessity of "burn it all down" tactics is the women's suffrage movement. While many are familiar with figures like Susan B. Anthony and Elizabeth Cady Stanton, whose strategies leaned toward negotiation and legal reform, fewer are aware of the radical tactics employed by suffragists like Alice Paul and the Silent Sentinels. These women picketed the White House during World War I, refusing to remain silent despite accusations of unpatriotism. They were arrested, imprisoned, and subjected to brutal treatment, including forced feeding during hunger strikes. Their actions were not polite, but they were effective. They forced the nation to confront the hypocrisy of fighting for democracy abroad while denying it to women at home.

Modern movements have also shown the power of disruption. The Black Lives Matter protests that erupted after the murder of George Floyd in 2020 were not civil in the traditional sense, they were loud, they were disruptive, and they demanded attention. Critics decried the protests as chaotic, but chaos was the point. The system that allowed George Floyd to be murdered in broad daylight was built on the illusion of order, an order that prioritized property over people, power over justice. The protests shattered that illusion, forcing the nation to reckon with the reality of systemic racism and police brutality.

The 4B Movement draws inspiration from these examples, recognizing that civility is a trap. The first step Burn is both figurative and literal. It is about setting fire to the illusions that keep us compliant, from the myth of bipartisan compromise to the fantasy that change can come without confrontation. Bipartisanship, in particular, is one of the most persistent lies of American politics. We are told that the two-party system can work if only we find common ground, but what common ground can exist between those who seek justice and those who seek to maintain oppression? Compromise is not possible when one side's starting point is the denial of basic human rights.

Burning these illusions requires more than rhetoric; it requires action. It means refusing to play by the rules of a system designed to keep us losing. It means disrupting the mechanisms of power, from corporate greed to legislative gridlock, and exposing the hypocrisy of those who preach unity while perpetuating division. The 4B Movement's call to Burn is not a call to destroy for destruction's sake, it is a call to clear the ground for something new. It is a rejection of civility as a strategy and a recognition that true progress requires confrontation.

The power of burning lies in its ability to create clarity. When the illusions are stripped away, what remains is the truth. The truth of systemic injustice, of unchecked greed, of entrenched inequality. Burning is not comfortable, it is raw, painful, and necessary. It forces us to confront the reality of the systems we live under and to imagine what might take their place. The act of burning is not just about destruction; it is about transformation. It is about creating the space for something better to rise from the ashes.

This philosophy has already begun to take root in communities across the country. Activists are rejecting the traditional playbook of polite appeals and instead embracing tactics that force attention and demand accountability. From labor strikes to direct action protests, these movements are disrupting the status quo and challenging the narratives that have long justified inequality. They are burning the lie that progress must be slow, that injustice must be tolerated, that those in power must be spared discomfort.

Burning the illusions of civility and compromise is not easy. It requires courage, resilience, and a willingness to be unpopular. It means standing firm in the face of criticism, even from those who claim to share your goals but balk at your methods. But history shows that this is the only way to create real change. The suffragists, the civil rights activists, the revolutionaries, they all faced backlash, and they all succeeded because they refused to be deterred.

The 4B Movement understands that burning is just the beginning. It is the spark that sets the stage for the other steps: Ban, Boycott, and Build. But without that spark, without the willingness to challenge the lies that sustain the status quo, no progress is possible. Burning is not just an act of destruction, it is an act of creation, of making space for a future that is equitable, just, and free.

As the flames rise, so too does the determination of those who refuse to accept the world as it is. The act of burning is not just about tearing down what exists; it is about lighting the way to what could be. And in that light lies the promise of a better tomorrow.

If the first part of the 4B Movement is about burning down illusions and exposing the lies that keep oppressive systems intact, the next phase of this burning is an unapologetic confrontation with power itself. Burn doesn't stop at rhetoric; it demands action, direct, unrelenting, and fearless. It isn't about playing the game better; it's about recognizing the game is rigged and flipping the table over. The lie that power will concede anything without a fight is perhaps the most dangerous of all, and the 4B Movement understands that to burn the system's illusions is to challenge its very foundations.

Let's be clear: the system was never designed to work for everyone. The founding principles of American democracy, celebrated with such fervor, were inherently exclusionary. The Constitution's lofty promises of equality were written by men who owned other humans as property and denied women any semblance of autonomy. The myth that the system can be fixed by simply asking those in power to act in good faith is a smokescreen. The system doesn't break, it functions exactly as intended, protecting wealth, power, and privilege while marginalizing everyone else. To burn is to reject this premise entirely, to stop patching up a foundation built on exploitation and start imagining something radically new.

Movements throughout history have shown that change comes when people disrupt the machinery of oppression, not when they wait for it to grind to a halt on its own. Take the Haitian Revolution, one of the most radical and transformative movements in history. The enslaved people of Haiti didn't ask for freedom; they took it, overthrowing one of the most powerful colonial empires in the world and establishing the first free Black republic. Their struggle was brutal, their resistance uncompromising, and their victory world-changing. The lesson is clear: those in power will not relinquish it willingly, and politeness has no place in the face of systemic oppression.

Another example can be found in the Stonewall Riots of 1969, a turning point for LGBTQ+ rights in the United States. These riots weren't planned or orderly; they were a spontaneous eruption of rage against decades of police harassment and societal rejection. The activists who fought back that night weren't concerned with civility, they were fighting for their lives. Stonewall became a spark that ignited a global movement, reminding the world that liberation doesn't come from waiting for permission but from demanding it.

Closer to our time, the Arab Spring demonstrated the power of collective defiance. In country after country, ordinary people took to the streets, challenging entrenched dictatorships and risking everything for a chance at freedom. These uprisings were chaotic, unpredictable, and often incomplete, but they showed the world what happens when people refuse to accept the inevitability of their oppression. Burning the lie that systems of power are immutable is a revolutionary act, one that requires not just courage but a deep belief in the possibility of change.

The 4B Movement draws strength from these lessons, understanding that burning isn't about destruction for its own sake, it's about clearing the ground for something better. The illusions of civility, bipartisanship, and incremental progress are not just obstacles; they are weapons wielded by those in power to keep the rest of us in line. Burning them means rejecting the idea that progress must be slow, that change must be negotiated, and that justice must wait. It means acknowledging that the system as it exists is unsalvageable and that the only way forward is through radical transformation.

Burning also means confronting the deeply ingrained narratives that justify inequality. The myth of the American Dream, for example, has long been used to placate those left behind by the system. It promises that hard work and determination will lead to success, ignoring the structural barriers that ensure wealth and opportunity remain concentrated in the hands of the few. The lie of meritocracy is another illusion that must be burned. It insists that success is a result of talent and effort, conveniently ignoring the role of privilege, connections, and systemic bias. These narratives are not just false, they are dangerous, convincing people to blame themselves for their struggles rather than the system that created them.

One of the most insidious illusions is the idea that the system can be reformed from within. While incremental progress is often necessary in the short term, the belief that deep, structural change can come from polite negotiation with those in power is a fantasy. The reality is that the system's gatekeepers have no interest in dismantling the very structures that maintain their power. They will offer compromises, symbolic victories, and token gestures, but they will never willingly cede the ground needed for true equality. Burning this illusion means refusing to be placated by half-measures and demanding nothing less than systemic overhaul.

The movement also recognizes that burning is not just about tearing down, it is about lighting the way forward. It's about creating the conditions for a new society to emerge, one built on principles of justice, equity, and solidarity. Burning the old means making space for the new, and that requires imagination as well as action. The flames of resistance must be guided by a vision of what comes next, a vision that prioritizes people over profit, communities over corporations, and liberation over control. The resistance to the 4B Movement's philosophy of burning is, of course, fierce.

Those who benefit from the current system will fight tooth and nail to preserve it, using every tool at their disposal to discredit, silence, and crush those who challenge their power. They will frame the movement as radical, dangerous, and even violent, conveniently ignoring the violence inherent in the systems they defend. They will invoke the language of civility, urging protesters to calm down and engage in "constructive dialogue," all while continuing to pass laws, hoard wealth, and increase inequality.

Burning means refusing to play this game, rejecting the terms set by those who have no interest in fairness, and creating new terms. Burning also means confronting the discomfort that comes with challenging deeply held beliefs. For many, the idea that the system is irredeemable is difficult to accept. It's easier to believe that progress is slow but inevitable, that justice will prevail if we simply wait long enough. But history shows otherwise.

Progress is not inevitable, it is the result of struggle, sacrifice, and the willingness to burn down what no longer serves us. Accepting this reality requires a level of discomfort that many are reluctant to face, but it is only by confronting this discomfort that true change becomes possible.

The 4B Movement's call to burn is not about destruction for its own sake. It is about transformation. It is about recognizing that the systems we live under are not broken, they are functioning exactly as designed, and that design is the problem. Burning means rejecting the lies that keep us compliant, the myths that keep us divided, and the narratives that justify oppression. It means creating the conditions for a new society to emerge, one that is not built on the ashes of the old but rises from them.

Chapter 4~BAN
Ban Everything They Love

The first rule of engagement with those who wield bans as weapons is this: meet them where they are, and then escalate. If they ban our books, we ban their tax exemptions. If they ban abortion, we ban their access to global platforms. The 4B Movement's second pillar Ban is a calculated strategy of direct retaliation, a refusal to play nice with those who legislate cruelty and demand civility in return. Banning isn't about pettiness; it's about leveling the playing field and using the same tools of power to hold the oppressors accountable. It is about showing that the weapons they use to control can also be turned against them, and that their monopolization of bans and boycotts is over.

The hypocrisy of their bans is impossible to ignore. When they ban books, it isn't about protecting children, it's about controlling narratives. The books they target are not random; they are calculated. Stories by and about marginalized communities, histories that challenge whitewashed myths, and texts that explore gender and identity are consistently their focus. They claim these bans are about shielding young minds from obscenity, but the real obscenity is the erasure of truths that don't align with their narrow worldview. The act of banning books isn't just an attack on free expression; it's a declaration of war on the stories and voices they fear.

And if they fear books, we should ask: what else do they fear? The 4B Movement recognizes that their vulnerabilities go beyond literature. Tax exemptions, for example, have long been a sacred cow for the institutions they rely on to spread their message. Churches that engage in political lobbying under the guise of faith, think tanks masquerading as non-profits, and massive corporations with charitable fronts all enjoy the benefits of tax exemptions while working to dismantle our rights. These privileges are not just undeserved, they are dangerous. By banning their tax exemptions, we expose their hypocrisy and cut off a vital lifeline of their influence.

It's not just about taxes; it's about platforms, too. Far-right groups thrive on access to global audiences, using social media, conferences, and financial systems to spread their agenda. They weaponize platforms like Twitter, Facebook, and YouTube to amplify disinformation and target marginalized communities. They rely on international banking systems to fund their operations, moving money across borders with little oversight. But access to these platforms is a privilege, not a right. When they ban abortion, when they ban queer representation, when they ban books, the response must be to ban their access to these same systems. Cut off their megaphones. Deny them the global reach they've weaponized against us.

History has shown the power of bans and boycotts as tools of resistance. The Montgomery Bus Boycott, one of the defining moments of the Civil Rights Movement, wasn't just about transportation, it was about economic power. By refusing to ride buses, Black Americans in Montgomery disrupted the system that relied on their labor and patronage. The boycott was a financial blow to the city and a moral blow to segregation. It demonstrated that withholding economic participation can be a powerful form of protest, one that forces oppressors to reckon with the consequences of their actions.

The 4B Movement draws on this legacy, using bans and boycotts as a form of direct retaliation. When they pass laws that strip away rights, we target the corporations that fund their campaigns. When they suppress queer voices, we refuse to support the platforms that enable their erasure. When they ban abortion, we work to cut off their access to the global networks that make their policies possible. These actions are not just symbolic, they are strategic. They disrupt the flow of power and resources that sustain their agenda, forcing them to feel the consequences of their cruelty.

Of course, retaliation through bans and boycotts isn't without its challenges. It requires coordination, persistence, and a willingness to withstand backlash. The forces we are up against are deeply entrenched, with access to resources and allies that make them formidable opponents. But the power of collective action should not be underestimated. When we act together, our impact is exponential. Banning their platforms, funding, and privileges is not something we can do individually, it is a collective effort, one that requires all of us to recognize our power as consumers, voters, and activists.

Banning is also about exposing the cracks in their armor. When we challenge their tax exemptions, we force them to defend the indefensible: their use of public subsidies to fund private oppression. When we ban their platforms, we expose their reliance on systems they claim to despise. Their ideology is built on a foundation of contradictions, and banning brings those contradictions to the surface. It forces them to confront the hypocrisy at the core of their movement, and it forces their supporters to reckon with the reality of what they are enabling.

One of the most effective ways to ban their influence is through divestment. The fossil fuel divestment movement, for example, has shown how targeting the financial lifelines of oppressive industries can create real change. By pressuring universities, pension funds, and other institutions to divest from fossil fuels, activists have both reduced the industry's access to capital and shifted the narrative around climate change. The same approach can be applied to far-right organizations and the corporations that support them. By identifying the networks of money and influence that sustain their agenda and pressuring institutions to divest, we can weaken their grip on power.

But banning is not just about cutting off resources, it's about creating alternatives. When we ban their books, we don't just stop buying from their publishers; we support independent bookstores and authors who tell the stories they fear. When we ban their platforms, we build our own, creating spaces for free expression and community that cannot be co-opted by hate. When we ban their funding sources, we invest in movements and organizations that work toward justice. Banning is not just a rejection of what exists; it is an affirmation of what could be.

The art of banning is in its precision. It's not about indiscriminate destruction; it's about targeting the structures and systems that uphold oppression. It's about understanding where their power comes from and cutting it off at the source. It's about refusing to participate in systems that harm us and building new systems that reflect our values. Banning is not a passive act, it is a declaration of agency, a refusal to accept the status quo, and a commitment to creating a better world.

The 4B Movement's approach to banning is unapologetic. It recognizes that those who wield bans as weapons cannot complain when those weapons are turned against them. They have banned our books, our voices, and our rights. Now, we ban their privileges, their platforms, and their power. And in doing so, we reclaim the tools of resistance and turn them into instruments of liberation.

In the face of systemic oppression, where traditional avenues of protest are either co-opted or ignored, the need for radical tactics becomes undeniable. The 4B Movement's call to ban isn't simply a strategy, it's a philosophy. A philosophy that rejects incremental change and the idea that systems of power can be gently reformed through polite requests or civil debate. No, the history of social movements has shown that true change requires direct confrontation, strategic dismantling, and the systematic erosion of the resources that prop up unjust systems. To ban is to say, "no more," and to act on that declaration with a clear and purposeful strategy.

The second part of the 4B Movement's playbook Ban is born from this understanding. It is about stripping the pillars that uphold an unjust system of its power, one piece at a time. And when we look at the tactics of those in power, it becomes clear: they use bans and boycotts to protect their interests, silence dissent, and preserve their control. Why, then, should we not turn those same tactics against them? Why should we stand by while they strip away our rights, ban our stories, and erase our history, without using the very same weapons to disrupt their monopoly on power?

If they ban books, we ban their tax exemptions. If they ban abortion, we ban their access to global platforms. If they seek to control reproductive rights, we control their economic resources, their media presence, and their political influence. If they attempt to stifle free expression, we will build new avenues for expression that cannot be co-opted, and we will dismantle their ability to suppress. Banning their access to tax exemptions, to platforms, and to influence is more than a statement, it is a clear and unequivocal message: we will not be complicit, and we will not cooperate with systems of oppression.

There's a dark irony in the way institutions and individuals that have shaped America's conservative policies have benefitted from tax exempt status. Churches, particularly those that engage in political lobbying, have long been able to use their status to influence elections, fund far-right political candidates, and legislate against reproductive and civil rights without any accountability. These institutions, instead

50

of being a sanctuary for the vulnerable, have become beacons of political power for those who wish to dismantle the very fabric of our democracy. Churches have long since abandoned their original call to serve the oppressed, focusing instead on cultivating wealth and influence. As they gather resources, they perpetuate policies that directly harm the most marginalized members of society.

So, if they are willing to use their tax-exempt status to manipulate, we must counter with a refusal to accept it. When you dig into the financials of the churches that push far-right policies, it's clear they've created empires, not houses of worship. And it's time we put an end to that empire-building, which is accomplished through the exploitation of public resources, and in turn, fuels the very policies that harm us. Banning tax exemptions for organizations that engage in political lobbying is a direct, necessary response. Their tax breaks allow them to funnel money into policies that strip away basic human rights, from reproductive health care to gender equality, to LGBTQ+ rights. By targeting their access to these exemptions, we cut off the financial lifeblood of their influence.

Take a closer look at how this plays out in real life: organizations like the Family Research Council and Focus on the Family are not small, quiet groups operating from basements, they have a vast, multi-million-dollar budget. They are able to hire lobbyists, fund political candidates, and run media campaigns that shape public opinion. This power is fueled by their tax-exempt status. By denying them these privileges, we create an undeniable financial and political chokehold on their ability to spread their oppressive agenda.

Next, let's look at the case of banning access to platforms. Far-right groups thrive on global platforms, think social media networks, news outlets, and entertainment platforms. They use these platforms to spread their ideologies, recruit supporters, and reinforce their grip on power. Facebook, Twitter, and YouTube, among others, have allowed hate speech, disinformation, and white nationalist rhetoric to flourish. While these platforms have occasionally cracked down on some extreme content, their actions have been far too little, too late. Meanwhile, far-right figures continue to make millions off their presence on these networks, from selling products to amassing followers who support their extremist views.

The 4B Movement's response to this is clear: ban their access to these global platforms. This is not about censorship, it's about holding platforms accountable for the hate they allow to spread. When you allow extremists to flood the public sphere with messages of hate, violence, and division, you are complicit in the destruction of democratic values. No more. These platforms have been complicit in the destruction of social cohesion and public discourse. By banning the far-right from these platforms, we deny them the megaphone that they have used to manipulate millions of people, radicalizing them and turning them into pawns in their quest for power.

But banning their access to global platforms is not just about cutting off their ability to spread hate, it's about giving rise to alternative spaces that foster inclusivity and mutual respect. Instead of allowing their rhetoric to dominate the discourse, we should create platforms that center diverse voices, voices of marginalized communities, voices of resistance, voices of love. We can and should build spaces that elevate the narratives of those who have long been silenced by the powers that be.

Another key tactic in this strategy of retaliation is the boycott. Boycotts have long been an essential tool for social movements fighting for justice. They provide a way to hit the powerful where it hurts most, through their profits. The Montgomery Bus Boycott, which played a crucial role in the Civil Rights Movement, is the most famous example. But it wasn't the only one. The boycott is an act of refusal, refusing to support businesses, corporations, and organizations that profit from injustice. If they refuse to respect our rights, we refuse to respect their profits.

Take, for instance, the corporate behemoths that fund the far-right agenda through political donations and lobbying. Companies like Koch Industries, ExxonMobil, and others use their immense resources to back politicians who champion the policies that dismantle our rights. These corporations push for tax cuts for the ultra-wealthy, deregulation of industries that harm the environment, and policies that strip workers of their rights. These actions are driven by profit and fueled by the unchecked political influence of these companies. The 4B Movement calls for a boycott of companies that profit from oppression. If they contribute to the oppression of marginalized communities, then they should not be supported by the very people they seek to harm.

Boycotts, like bans, aren't just symbolic, they're strategic. When millions of people choose not to spend their money on companies that support harmful policies, it sends a powerful message. The impact is financial, cultural, and political. In the same way that divesting from fossil fuels has been a powerful tool in the fight against climate change, boycotts of corporations that fund the far-right agenda can force companies to rethink their alliances. And just as we cut off their access to tax exemptions, we can cut off their funding through strategic boycotts.

While these actions are necessary, they are not without consequences. The forces we are up against are powerful, deeply entrenched, and they fight dirty. We will face smear campaigns, misinformation, and pushback from the corporations and politicians whose interests we threaten. But history has shown that movements built on righteous fury and strategic action can, and will, win. It is not enough to ask for change; we must demand it, through every channel available to us. The 4B Movement's focus on banning, boycotting, and strategically cutting off their access to resources is a way of saying, loud and clear: we won't be complicit in our own oppression, and we will not sit back while they dismantle our rights and our future.

The fight will be hard, but the path forward is clear. If they ban everything we love, we will ban everything they cherish. And we will keep building, from the ground up, until our world is one where justice, equity, and love are the foundations upon which we build. The time to act is now, and the tools of resistance, banning, boycotting, and disrupting, are already in our hands. Together, we will not only take back what is ours; we will create something far better in its place.

Chapter 5~BAN
Language is a Weapon

Words have power. The meanings we attach to words shape the world we live in. When those in power control language, they control reality. This has been the cornerstone of every authoritarian regime, every ideological movement, and every system of oppression: the ability to manipulate the meaning of words, to redefine concepts, and to shape narratives. The far-right and the Christian nationalist movements have long understood this, using language not just as a means of communication but as a weapon. They've redefined "freedom," "family values," and "morality" in ways that serve their own interests, distorting their true meanings and weaponizing them to maintain power and suppress dissent.

The first battle in the war for language is to take back the words they've stolen and to restore their true, empowering meanings. Words like "freedom," "family values," and "morality" have been co-opted by the far-right to serve a narrow, exclusionary agenda. The 4B Movement recognizes that in order to win the war, we must reclaim these words and use them for the forces of justice and equality. It's time to take the language back from those who have corrupted it and use it to reshape our world.

Freedom

The word "freedom" has become one of the most weaponized terms in the far-right's lexicon. They have twisted it to mean the freedom to oppress others, the freedom to deny basic rights to marginalized communities, the freedom to ignore science, and the freedom to hoard resources. Under their definition, freedom is a shield for the wealthy and powerful to avoid accountability, while those at the bottom are told to pull themselves up by their bootstraps. Freedom, as they define it, is a privilege, not a right, a privilege that belongs to the powerful few and is never extended to the oppressed.

But true freedom is not about the ability to dominate others. True freedom is about autonomy, equality, and the dismantling of the systems that perpetuate injustice. It is the freedom to make choices about one's own body, one's own life, and one's own future without fear of discrimination or violence. True freedom means access to education, healthcare, economic opportunity, and justice. It means the freedom to live as one truly is, without fear of persecution for one's identity. It means liberation for all, not just the privileged.

We must reclaim the meaning of freedom and push back against the far-right's twisted interpretation. This means framing freedom not as the right to dominate, but as the right to live in a just, equitable, and inclusive society. The freedom to love whom you choose, to be free from discrimination, to exist in a world where your rights are protected and your humanity is respected. When we reclaim the word freedom, we reject their authoritarian version and replace it with one that affirms the dignity and rights of all people, regardless of race, gender, sexual orientation, or economic status.

Family Values

"Family values" is another word that has been hijacked and distorted by the far-right. What was once a concept rooted in the belief that families should be supported and cared for has been twisted into a tool for exclusion and control. Today, when politicians invoke "family values," what they really mean is a return to traditional gender roles, the erasure of LGBTQ+ identities, the subjugation of women, and the reinforcement of patriarchal systems that have long harmed marginalized communities. Under their interpretation, family values are about maintaining a rigid, heteronormative standard that excludes anyone who doesn't fit into their narrow vision of what a family should look like.

But "family values" should never be synonymous with oppression. True family values mean supporting all families, regardless of structure or makeup. It means fighting for the economic, healthcare, and educational policies that help families thrive, whether they are headed by single parents, same-sex couples, or multigenerational households. Family values mean ensuring that everyone has access to paid leave, affordable childcare, and protections from discrimination in the workplace. It means valuing children by ensuring they grow up in safe, loving environments with the resources they need to succeed.

To reclaim family values, we must embrace a vision of family that is diverse, inclusive, and supportive. A vision of family that prioritizes the well-being of all its members, not just those who fit into a narrow, outdated ideal. Family values should be about love, support, and equality, not about imposing one vision of the family on everyone. We must use the term to demand policies that provide families with the resources they need to thrive, from universal healthcare to affordable housing to an economy that works for everyone.

Morality

The far-right has also weaponized the term "morality." They have used it as a cudgel to justify laws that discriminate against women, LGBTQ+ individuals, immigrants, and people of color. For them, morality is about control, control over people's bodies, control over people's sexualities, control over the way people choose to live their lives. They use the term to impose their own narrow, religiously-infused values on everyone, claiming moral superiority while simultaneously defending systems that perpetuate violence, inequality, and injustice.

But true morality is not about imposing one set of beliefs on others, it's about compassion, justice, and fairness. True morality means standing up for the oppressed, fighting against systems of inequality, and ensuring that everyone is treated with dignity and respect. It means recognizing the inherent value of every person, regardless of their race, gender, sexual orientation, or background, and ensuring that they have the opportunity to live a full, healthy life free from discrimination. Morality should be about empathy, not judgment; about building systems that lift people up, not tear them down.

To reclaim morality, we must shift the narrative from one of exclusion to one of inclusion, from one of condemnation to one of compassion. We must challenge the idea that morality is about controlling people's choices and instead embrace a vision of morality rooted in justice, equality, and human rights. The fight for true morality means standing up for the rights of women to control their own bodies, fighting for LGBTQ+ rights, advocating for racial justice, and demanding that our institutions uphold the dignity and humanity of every person. True morality means caring for the most vulnerable

among us, ensuring that no one is left behind, and working toward a
society that reflects the values of justice, love, and respect.

The Orwellian Nature of Doublespeak

The far-right's use of language is not just about manipulation, it's
about control. George Orwell's concept of "Newspeak" in *1984* is
perhaps the most extreme example of language as a tool of control. In
Orwell's dystopia, language is stripped of its meaning, and words are
redefined to serve the purposes of the state. In the same way, the far-
right has redefined words like freedom, family values, and morality to
suit their agenda, erasing the true meaning of these terms and
replacing them with hollow, empty slogans that are used to justify
their actions.

This Orwellian doublespeak is a hallmark of far-right rhetoric. They
use terms like "freedom" to justify stripping away rights, "family
values" to restrict who can marry and raise children, and "morality"
to defend oppressive laws that harm the most vulnerable. But beneath
the surface, these words have been hollowed out, emptied of their true
meaning, and repurposed as tools for domination and control. The 4B
Movement understands that we must not only reclaim these words
but also expose the lies behind them. We must use the very language
they have distorted to call out their hypocrisy and to reassert the true
values that these words represent.

The 4B Movement's approach to language is not just about
reclaiming words, it's about reclaiming meaning. It's about refusing to
allow the powerful to define our reality through their twisted use of
language. It's about recognizing that language is a tool of
empowerment, a way to tell our stories, define our values, and shape
the world around us. When we use language to tell the truth, to
expose the lies of the powerful, and to assert our collective power, we
begin to take back control of the narrative.

As we continue to challenge the far-right's use of language, we must
also create new narratives. We must write the stories that reflect the
world we want to build, a world where freedom, family, and morality
are grounded in justice, equality, and love. We must build a language
that speaks to the dignity of every person, that recognizes the

humanity of those who have been marginalized, and that resists the oppression of those who would use words as weapons.

By taking back the language, we take back the power. It is time to stop allowing our words to be co-opted, twisted, and weaponized. It is time to use language for liberation, for truth, and for justice.

The fight for language is not merely academic; it is the heart of the struggle for power. When words are hijacked, twisted, and weaponized by those in power, they shape how we think, act, and engage with the world. They mold our perceptions of right and wrong, normal and abnormal, and acceptable and unacceptable. The far-right has long understood this. By controlling the meaning of key words, "freedom," "family values," "morality," they manipulate the very language we use to describe our collective reality. It's time to change that. It's time to expose their linguistic deception, reclaim these words for their true meanings, and build a new language of justice, equality, and liberation.

The War on "Freedom"

One of the most abused words in the far-right's lexicon is "freedom." Under their definition, freedom is an unbridled privilege that allows the rich to grow richer and the powerful to maintain their grip on society. They weaponize freedom to defend an economic system that perpetuates inequality, while claiming that those who demand economic justice, healthcare, and reproductive rights are "threatening freedom." This twisted logic has to be challenged head-on.

Freedom is not about an unchecked ability to do whatever you want at the expense of others. True freedom is about opportunity, equality, and justice for all. It's about freedom from oppression, freedom from poverty, and freedom from discrimination. It's the freedom to choose one's future, without being chained to a system that favors the wealthy and powerful.

The 4B Movement's mission is clear: reclaim freedom for the people. We reclaim freedom from the corporate interests that use it to hoard wealth while paying minimal taxes. We reclaim freedom from politicians who strip away healthcare, deny women control over their bodies, and abandon the most vulnerable in our society. True freedom means creating a system that works for all people, not just the few.

Freedom isn't something that can be handed down; it must be fought for, reclaimed, and defended. The 4B Movement's strategy starts with rejecting the far-right's concept of freedom and replacing it with one that affirms equality, economic justice, and universal rights. We will no longer allow them to dictate the terms of freedom; we will create a new vision, one where freedom is a collective pursuit, not a tool of domination.

Reclaiming "Family Values"

The term "family values" has been hijacked by the far-right as a code for reinforcing heteronormative, patriarchal ideals that exclude anyone who doesn't fit their narrow definition of what a family should look like. When politicians invoke "family values," what they really mean is the preservation of a particular vision of the family, one where women are subservient to men, children are expected to conform to gender roles, and LGBTQ+ people are excluded entirely.

But family values are not about enforcing one rigid definition of family, they are about ensuring that all families have access to the resources, support, and opportunities they need to thrive. The truth is that family values should be about love, support, and mutual respect. A family doesn't need to conform to any single model to be valid. Families can look different, and they can be strong, loving, and full of promise.

The 4B Movement is committed to reclaiming family values for everyone. We will no longer allow the far-right to use this term as a weapon to justify discrimination and marginalization. Instead, we will center policies that support all families, whether single-parent households, same-sex couples, or multi-generational families. Family values mean creating a society where families can thrive, where there is universal healthcare, affordable childcare, paid family leave, and an economy that works for everyone, not just the wealthy few.

By reclaiming family values, we challenge the far-right's narrow vision and expand the definition of family to include everyone. We will push for policies that reflect the true values of family: care, protection, and equal rights. It's time to stop letting the far-right define what a family is, and instead, create a world where all families are supported, loved, and valued.

Reclaiming "Morality"

Perhaps one of the most insidious ways the far-right has distorted language is through the term "morality." They have used this word to justify policies that harm vulnerable populations, including restrictions on reproductive rights, bans on LGBTQ+ rights, and the dismantling of social safety nets. In their world, morality is about control, controlling who can marry, who can love, who can access healthcare, and who gets to live with dignity.

True morality, however, is not about controlling others; it is about empathy, justice, and fairness. It is about lifting people up, not tearing them down. It is about fighting for a world where everyone has the opportunity to live freely, without fear of discrimination or violence. Morality, at its core, is about caring for others, ensuring that all people, regardless of their race, gender, or socioeconomic status, are treated with dignity and respect.

The 4B Movement is working to reclaim morality from the far-right and redefine it in terms of justice, equality, and love. We will no longer allow them to claim that morality is about denying people their rights. We will stand firm in our belief that morality is about fighting for the well-being of all, not just the privileged few. Our vision of morality is one where we support the most vulnerable, where we ensure everyone has access to the resources they need to thrive, and where we build a society that prioritizes care over control.

Counteracting Orwellian Doublespeak

In George Orwell's *1984*, language is used as a tool of totalitarian control, a means of manipulating the truth and creating a reality that serves the state. Orwell's concept of "Newspeak" is a language designed to restrict thought, to erase the possibility of rebellion, and to limit the scope of discourse to only what the ruling power approves. While we are not yet living in a world as extreme as Orwell's dystopia, the far-right's use of doublespeak bears striking similarities.

When they use terms like "freedom" or "morality," they are not speaking the truth, they are creating a version of reality that suits their agenda. They use language to obscure their true intentions, to dress up cruelty as compassion, and to justify oppression as righteousness. They frame economic inequality as a meritocracy, racial injustice as "law and order," and the destruction of the environment as "progress."

But the 4B Movement understands the power of language, and we will not let their doublespeak go unchallenged. We will expose the contradictions in their language and reveal the truth behind their rhetoric. We will use language to create a new narrative, one that centers justice, equality, and liberation. We will build our own version of reality, a reality where everyone has a voice, where the truth is not obscured by false narratives, and where power is held accountable for its words and deeds.

One way to fight back against Orwellian doublespeak is to reframe their language. When they say "pro-life," we must point out that their policies are not pro-life, they are pro-birth, and they fail to protect the lives of the vulnerable after birth. When they talk about "family values," we must expose their definition as narrow and exclusionary, and demand that all families be recognized and supported. When they talk about "freedom," we must call out the fact that their version of freedom is really about privileging the few and oppressing the many.

Reframing language requires precision, but it also requires persistence. We must consistently challenge their use of language, exposing the gaps between their rhetoric and their actions. The more we do this, the more we can build a new narrative, one that emphasizes justice, compassion, and equality for all. By calling out the Orwellian doublespeak of the far-right, we take the first step in dismantling their control over the discourse and reclaiming the power of language for ourselves.

Creating a New Language of Liberation

The 4B Movement's vision of language is not just reactive; it is proactive. We are not just responding to the far-right's language; we are creating our own. A language of liberation is one that recognizes the humanity of all people and refuses to be complicit in systems of oppression. It is a language that names injustice for what it is and calls for action to address it. It is a language that elevates voices of resistance and celebrates the diversity and richness of our world.

We create this new language by speaking the truth, by refusing to accept the false narratives imposed upon us, and by reimagining a future where justice is the norm, not the exception. This new language is one of solidarity, one that builds bridges between communities and emphasizes collective action. It is a language that embraces intersectionality, recognizing the interconnectedness of struggles for racial, gender, economic, and environmental justice. It is a language that speaks of hope, resilience, and the possibility of change.

In this fight for language, we must recognize that words are not just symbols, they are actions. They shape our world, influence our thinking, and determine the policies we enact. To change the world, we must change the words we use. The 4B Movement's commitment to reclaiming language is a commitment to reclaiming power itself. By wielding language as a tool of resistance, we challenge the narratives of the powerful and create new possibilities for the future.

Chapter 6~BAN
Fighting Fire With Lawsuits

The law is a double-edged sword. On one hand, it has the power to uphold justice, protect rights, and ensure fairness in society. On the other, it can be twisted and manipulated to perpetuate inequality, suppress dissent, and enforce the will of the powerful. In today's political climate, where the far-right is relentlessly pushing an agenda that seeks to strip away the rights of marginalized communities and reinforce authoritarian control, one of the most potent tools of resistance we have left is the court system. Lawsuits, legal challenges, and court orders have become central to the battle for justice, and it is time for us to fight fire with lawsuits.

The courts are where policies are challenged, where laws are tested, and where the fate of entire communities can be decided. It's not enough to simply protest, organize, or vote, we must also be ready to litigate, to use the legal system as a weapon to block and overturn harmful policies. By strategically leveraging the courts, we can chip away at the far-right's agenda, hold powerful entities accountable, and build a legal foundation that protects civil rights, democracy, and human dignity. The court system is not perfect, but when used strategically, it remains one of the most powerful tools in the resistance toolkit.

Sue to Block: Challenging Harmful Policies

One of the most immediate ways to fight back against the far-right agenda is through lawsuits that block harmful policies before they can take effect. The far-right's strategy often involves pushing through extreme policies at the state or federal level with the support of conservative judges and lawmakers. Whether it's restrictions on reproductive rights, discriminatory laws targeting LGBTQ+ people, or efforts to dismantle voting rights, these policies can cause lasting harm if left unchecked. The good news is that the courts provide a powerful mechanism for blocking these policies before they can be fully implemented.

Litigating against harmful policies requires a strong legal strategy, and the first step is identifying the specific laws or executive orders that need to be challenged. This is where organizations like the ACLU, Planned Parenthood, and others come into play. These groups have extensive experience in using lawsuits to challenge policies that infringe on civil rights, reproductive rights, and social justice. By filing legal challenges, these organizations are able to seek injunctions or court orders that temporarily block harmful policies until they can be reviewed in full. These efforts can delay, weaken, or completely stop the implementation of harmful laws.

For instance, when the Trump administration sought to implement a "Muslim ban" that targeted immigrants from Muslim-majority countries, multiple legal challenges were filed almost immediately. The ACLU and other organizations were successful in obtaining temporary injunctions that blocked the implementation of the ban, forcing the courts to intervene and ultimately ruling that the policy was discriminatory and unconstitutional. The same strategies have been used in fighting back against anti-abortion laws, anti-transgender legislation, and efforts to limit voting rights.

In these cases, timing is everything. The sooner a lawsuit is filed, the sooner the courts can intervene and put a halt to the damage. By using the courts to block harmful policies, we buy time to organize, rally public support, and push for legislative action. Lawsuits can serve as a critical line of defense in the ongoing battle to protect rights and freedoms, particularly when legislative avenues are blocked by partisan gridlock or the influence of powerful interests.

Overwhelm Their Agenda: Using the Courts to Exhaust the System

Another way to fight fire with lawsuits is to use the legal system to overwhelm the far-right agenda, making it so difficult and costly for them to push their policies that they are forced to retreat. In this strategy, the goal is to flood the courts with legal challenges, lawsuits, and legal actions that disrupt the far-right's ability to implement their agenda. This isn't about winning every case (though we should aim to do that,) it's about creating a constant, overwhelming pressure that forces them to divert their resources and attention away from their agenda.

This approach has been effective in slowing down harmful policy changes, forcing the far-right to spend time and money defending their actions in court. Consider the ongoing legal battles surrounding abortion rights, for instance. The far-right has worked relentlessly to pass restrictive abortion laws at the state level, often seeking to chip away at the protections provided by Roe v. Wade. Each time a state passes one of these laws, it triggers multiple lawsuits, leading to lengthy court battles that ultimately delay the implementation of the laws. These legal battles force anti-choice groups to expend resources fighting in the courts, and they can ultimately create enough public and legal pressure to overturn the laws before they take full effect.

Similarly, efforts to restrict voting rights have been met with a flood of lawsuits, making it harder for the far-right to impose voter suppression laws. These cases often take years to resolve, and while the legal process drags on, it prevents these laws from having their intended impact. By strategically filing lawsuits that challenge every aspect of the far-right's agenda, we create a legal battlefield where they cannot advance their policies without being delayed, weakened, or blocked altogether. The sheer volume of legal actions forces them to expend energy and resources that could otherwise be used to push their agenda through other channels.

Legal overwhelm can also help expose the far-right's strategy and weaken their credibility. When these lawsuits flood the courts, they highlight the extreme and often unconstitutional nature of their policies. Legal victories in court can send powerful messages to the public and lawmakers, demonstrating that these policies are not just unpopular but legally untenable. This strategy relies on persistence, patience, and a collective commitment to using the courts to disrupt the far-right's agenda at every turn.

Organizations Leading the Way

There are already organizations doing the vital work of fighting the far-right's agenda through the court system. The ACLU (American Civil Liberties Union), Planned Parenthood, Lambda Legal, the NAACP Legal Defense and Educational Fund, and the Southern Poverty Law Center are just a few examples of groups that have been instrumental in challenging discriminatory laws, fighting for reproductive rights, and defending civil liberties in court. These organizations provide not only legal expertise but also the resources necessary to fight the far-right on the legal front.

The ACLU, for example, has been at the forefront of numerous high-profile cases, from defending the rights of immigrants facing deportation to challenging unconstitutional surveillance practices. The organization has been involved in dozens of lawsuits challenging voter suppression laws, discriminatory immigration policies, and attacks on LGBTQ+ rights. Through its extensive network of attorneys and supporters, the ACLU has become one of the most important players in the fight against the far-right's agenda.

Planned Parenthood, meanwhile, has been the leading organization in defending reproductive rights through the courts. Over the years, they have successfully challenged numerous state-level abortion bans and restrictions, ensuring that women's reproductive rights remain protected. Planned Parenthood's legal team is constantly involved in litigation aimed at blocking the implementation of unconstitutional laws that threaten access to abortion, contraception, and other reproductive health services. Their work has been instrumental in preserving access to safe and legal abortion in the face of growing opposition.

Lambda Legal has been a key player in advocating for LGBTQ+ rights, particularly in the area of anti-discrimination laws and marriage equality. The organization has been involved in some of the most landmark cases in LGBTQ+ civil rights, including the successful challenge to the Defense of Marriage Act (DOMA) and the fight for transgender rights. Lambda Legal's legal team is constantly working to expand protections for LGBTQ+ individuals, and their lawsuits have been a vital part of the movement toward full equality.

The NAACP Legal Defense and Educational Fund has long been an advocate for racial justice, working to dismantle discriminatory policies and fight back against voter suppression efforts. Their legal team has fought tirelessly to protect the Voting Rights Act and ensure that Black Americans can participate in the democratic process. Through lawsuits challenging discriminatory laws, the NAACP has been a central figure in the fight for racial equality in the U.S.

The Southern Poverty Law Center (SPLC) is another organization that uses the court system to fight back against hate and bigotry. The SPLC tracks hate groups and extremists, providing legal assistance to victims of discrimination, and filing lawsuits against those who perpetuate hate crimes. Their work has been crucial in holding white nationalist groups and other extremists accountable through the courts.

These organizations are already doing the heavy lifting in the fight against the far-right's agenda, and their work is essential to the resistance. By supporting these organizations, joining their efforts, and amplifying their legal battles, we can collectively increase the pressure on the far-right's agenda and hold those in power accountable. They show us how to strategically use the court system to block harmful policies, protect our rights, and challenge the status quo.

Lawsuits are not just tools for pushing back against harmful policies, they are instruments of disruption. In the ongoing fight against the far-right's agenda, the legal system serves as a powerful, albeit often underutilized, battleground. The 4B Movement, with its focus on strategic action, recognizes that litigation can slow, block, and even defeat policies designed to oppress and disenfranchise. It is a form of direct resistance that can chip away at the structures of power, expose the hypocrisy of those who wield it, and reshape public discourse.

Legal challenges work in tandem with direct action, organizing, and cultural shifts. They demand the attention of politicians, media outlets, and the public. When a lawsuit is filed, it often forces an issue into the spotlight, sometimes forcing lawmakers to address the constitutional and moral implications of their policies. Even when a case is lost, the process of going through the courts can create significant public pressure, resulting in legislative or societal change.

Strategic Lawsuits as a Weapon of Resistance

Strategic litigation doesn't just aim for victories in individual cases; it aims to set a legal precedent that can affect broader societal change. By using the legal system to fight back against harmful policies, the 4B Movement can establish a series of legal rulings that protect civil rights, curb abuses of power, and ensure that those who perpetuate injustice are held accountable. The far-right may hold significant power in state legislatures and the federal government, but the court system is still a site of struggle where the law, for all its flaws, can be a force for progressive change.

One key approach is to file lawsuits in response to the far-right's legislative actions, with the aim of blocking or delaying their implementation. In many cases, these lawsuits don't just stop a policy, they create the opportunity for public discourse, allowing the issue to be debated in courtrooms and the media, with public opinion often playing a significant role in the final outcome. For example, when the Trump administration attempted to institute a ban on transgender individuals in the military, lawsuits were filed immediately, and the case became a focal point for national debate. Eventually, the U.S. Supreme Court allowed the ban to proceed, but the long legal battle put the issue at the forefront of public discussion, ensuring that transgender rights continued to be an active point of contention in the national dialogue.

Similarly, lawsuits challenging voter suppression laws, such as those that restrict access to voting based on race, have provided an opportunity for activists and legal experts to illuminate the ways in which such laws disproportionately impact marginalized communities. The process of suing to block these laws often leads to a thorough examination of their intent and effect, providing a crucial opportunity to expose the discriminatory practices behind them.

The Role of Class-Action Lawsuits in Overwhelming Oppressive Systems

Class-action lawsuits are another key tool in challenging the far-right agenda. These lawsuits allow multiple individuals who have been similarly harmed by a policy or law to come together in one case, strengthening the legal challenge and making it harder for those in power to dismiss or ignore. Class-action suits have historically been used to challenge systemic injustices, from racial discrimination to labor exploitation, and they remain one of the most powerful legal mechanisms available to hold institutions accountable.

The potential impact of class-action lawsuits in the fight against the far-right is immense. Consider, for example, the way corporations and political organizations align themselves with far-right causes, often through funding, political lobbying, or legal loopholes. A class-action lawsuit that targets companies or individuals who benefit from far-right policies or who contribute to systems of inequality can not only challenge the specific policy in question but also raise awareness about the larger corporate and political structures that prop up these policies.

One successful example of this kind of legal resistance is the class-action lawsuits filed against employers who engage in discriminatory hiring practices or fail to protect employees from harassment. These cases, by putting pressure on corporations, have led to significant changes in the way businesses operate, forcing them to adopt more equitable policies and practices. The same principles can be applied to challenge harmful policies, whether it's a lawsuit targeting a company's role in perpetuating voter suppression or challenging corporate donations to far-right political action committees (PACs).

Litigation as a Tool for Protecting Reproductive Rights

One area where lawsuits have proven particularly powerful is in the fight for reproductive rights. The far-right has long sought to roll back abortion access and restrict reproductive freedoms, and they have been emboldened by a conservative judiciary that is increasingly sympathetic to their agenda. Yet, even in the face of this mounting threat, legal challenges have stalled or reversed many of the far-right's attempts to limit reproductive rights.

Organizations like Planned Parenthood, the Center for Reproductive Rights, and the ACLU have been at the forefront of this fight, using lawsuits to challenge abortion bans and restrictions at the state level. For example, when states like Texas and Mississippi passed restrictive abortion laws that would effectively eliminate access to abortion services, lawsuits were immediately filed to block these laws. These legal challenges forced courts to review the constitutionality of these laws, and in many cases, courts issued temporary injunctions that delayed or halted their enforcement.

These lawsuits, while often long and drawn-out, have been essential in ensuring that abortion access remains protected, even as the far-right attempts to overturn Roe v. Wade and impose draconian restrictions on reproductive rights. In the event of a ruling against abortion access, these lawsuits provide a means of appealing, and in some cases, overturning such decisions, creating an ongoing cycle of resistance.

One important lesson from these legal battles is that winning in the courts doesn't always require immediate success. Even in cases where the ultimate ruling may not go in favor of reproductive rights, the legal process itself can be a victory. It raises public awareness, galvanizes activists, and provides the foundation for continued advocacy and future legal challenges. Legal fights are not always quick wins; they are part of a broader, longer struggle to preserve and protect rights.

The Necessity of Building Legal Networks

While the ACLU, Planned Parenthood, and other legal organizations are critical in the fight against the far-right, it's important to recognize that they can't do this work alone. Successful legal challenges require not only skilled legal teams but also strong networks of activists, organizers, and community members who can lend their voices, their time, and their resources to support these efforts.

Building a robust legal infrastructure requires a combination of legal expertise and grassroots support. Activists must engage in litigation strategy, fundraising, and community outreach to support lawsuits. Legal battles can be expensive, and without the financial resources to fund these efforts, even the most well-meaning lawsuits can stall. That's why organizations like the ACLU and Planned Parenthood often rely on grassroots fundraising campaigns to fuel their legal battles.

Furthermore, as more and more states pass extreme anti-choice laws, organizing across state lines becomes essential. When states pass laws that are unconstitutional, organizations must work quickly to file lawsuits, appeal rulings, and ensure that these laws are blocked until they can be fully examined in the courts. National legal networks help ensure that these cases have the resources they need to be successful, and they also create a unified front of resistance against the far-right's agenda.

Examples of Legal Battles and the Importance of Persistence

In recent years, the fight for civil rights, voting rights, and reproductive justice has been marked by a growing number of legal battles that highlight both the power and limits of the legal system in resisting authoritarian agendas. These cases offer a glimpse into the strategies used by resistance groups and the hurdles they face as they use the courts to block harmful policies.

One of the most notable cases in the recent fight for voting rights was the legal challenge to North Carolina's voter ID law, which was passed in 2013 and aimed to suppress the votes of African Americans and other marginalized communities. The ACLU and other organizations immediately filed lawsuits challenging the law, arguing that it violated the Voting Rights Act of 1965. After years of litigation, the courts ruled that the law was discriminatory and ordered changes to the state's voting procedures. This legal victory was not only a win for North Carolina voters, but it also sent a message to other states that were considering similar voter suppression laws.

Similarly, when anti-transgender laws were passed in states like North Carolina, lawsuits were filed to challenge them. In the case of North Carolina's infamous "bathroom bill," the ACLU and Lambda Legal filed a lawsuit on behalf of transgender individuals who were being denied access to public restrooms that corresponded with their gender identity. The legal challenge resulted in a settlement that helped restore transgender rights in the state, and the issue of transgender rights became a central part of the national conversation.

These examples demonstrate the importance of persistence in legal battles. Lawsuits can take years to resolve, and the outcome is not always certain. But even in the face of setbacks, legal challenges force courts to engage with important issues and provide the space for public debate. Over time, these legal victories accumulate, creating a broader foundation for social change.

Chapter 7~BOYCOTT
The Tyranny of the Dollar

In the modern age, the battle for justice is not just fought with words or laws, it's fought with money. The dollar, in its insidious and pervasive nature, has become the most powerful tool in the hands of those who seek to maintain power. Corporations, through their massive financial resources and lobbying efforts, prop up the theocratic fascism that threatens to dismantle the hard-won civil rights and freedoms of the many in favor of the few. The far-right is not just a political movement, it is an economic force, one driven by the need to accumulate power through wealth, control, and domination. The corporate interests behind this movement must be exposed, their financial influence curtailed, and their power diminished. We must starve them.

For too long, these corporations have been allowed to operate with impunity, funneling money into political campaigns, think tanks, and lobbying efforts that push forward an agenda of hate, oppression, and inequality. They have funded the rise of Christian nationalism, helped to dismantle reproductive rights, and poured billions into efforts to suppress voting, limit healthcare access, and ensure that only the rich have a say in the shaping of society. These corporations operate with no accountability, unchallenged by a public more concerned with their consumer purchases than the political ideologies they fund. It is time to take the fight to their financial gates, starve their ability to manipulate the system, and demand that the corporate world be held accountable for its role in propping up tyranny.

The Corporate Giants Behind the Far-Right

The corporations funding theocratic fascism are not only vast in size but also in influence. They sit at the intersection of power, politics, and profit. Companies like Koch Industries, ExxonMobil, and Walmart, among others, funnel money into far-right think tanks, super PACs, and lobbying groups that push policies favorable to their bottom line. They fight to preserve an economic system built on the exploitation of workers, the extraction of resources, and the consolidation of power in the hands of the wealthy elite.

Take, for example, the Koch brothers and their vast network of political and corporate influence. Charles and David Koch, through their company Koch Industries, have spent billions funding libertarian and conservative causes, including opposition to environmental regulations, labor rights, and corporate taxes. Their political organizations, such as Americans for Prosperity, have been instrumental in funding right-wing political candidates and pushing policies that favor deregulation, lower taxes for the wealthy, and the dismantling of social safety nets. This is not just a political agenda, it is a corporate agenda, one designed to ensure that the wealthy stay wealthy, no matter the cost to society or the environment.

Then there's ExxonMobil, one of the world's largest oil and gas companies, whose influence stretches far beyond the boardroom. Exxon has spent decades funding climate change denial, lobbying against environmental protections, and pouring money into political campaigns that seek to suppress renewable energy initiatives. Their contributions to political candidates and groups that support the fossil fuel industry are vast, ensuring that their interests remain at the forefront of political agendas. Their pursuit of profit at the expense of the planet is only possible because of the financial power they wield, and that power must be challenged if we are to secure a just future for all.

Walmart, the largest retailer in the world, is another example of corporate influence at work. While many think of Walmart as a store that sells everything from groceries to electronics, behind the scenes, it is a company that has relentlessly fought to preserve its monopolistic grip on the retail market. Walmart's lobbying efforts have been aimed at weakening labor protections, fighting against increases in the minimum wage, and opposing any initiatives that might threaten its bottom line. The company has been a vocal supporter of far-right policies, including those that limit access to healthcare and voting, and has used its influence to push these agendas forward.

These corporations, along with many others, have used their financial power to fund the rise of the far-right agenda, supporting theocrats who are eager to enshrine conservative religious beliefs into law, and pushing for the dismantling of democratic processes that might challenge their dominance. They fund PACs, pay for advertising, and engage in legal lobbying efforts to ensure that policies are enacted that protect their financial interests, even when those policies harm the broader public. It is not just about politics, it's about profit. And it is time to starve them.

Divesting: Cutting Off the Financial Lifeblood

The first step in starving the corporations that fund theocratic fascism is to hit them where it hurts most: their wallets. Divestment is a powerful tool in the fight against corporate influence, particularly when it comes to corporations that fund harmful political causes. Divesting means removing investments from companies that support far-right agendas and redirecting those funds toward more ethical investments. It is a direct financial attack on the companies that fund oppression, but it is also a call to action that sends a message to corporations: If you want to continue profiting off the backs of the marginalized, you will be held accountable.

The divestment movement has seen successes in the past, particularly in the fight against apartheid in South Africa. In the 1980s, activists called on institutions, including universities, pension funds, and governments, to divest from companies doing business with the apartheid regime. The result was a massive withdrawal of financial support from companies that helped maintain the system of apartheid, ultimately forcing the regime to reconsider its policies. Divestment was not just a financial strategy, it was a moral strategy. It sent a clear message that certain policies and practices would not be tolerated, and it applied significant pressure to those in power to change.

Today, the 4B Movement must take a similar approach to divesting from corporations that fund theocratic fascism. This means identifying which companies are directly contributing to the far-right agenda and cutting off financial support. It involves encouraging investors, municipalities, universities, and pension funds to withdraw investments from companies like Koch Industries, ExxonMobil, and Walmart, and to redirect those funds toward more socially responsible companies. Divestment is about stripping away the financial power that allows these corporations to fund oppressive political agendas and creating a network of ethical investment that challenges the status quo.

Divestment also extends to individuals. If we are to starve the corporations that fund far-right movements, we must make conscious choices in where we spend our money. By boycotting companies that fund or support the far-right, we reduce their consumer base and make it financially untenable for them to continue to fund policies that harm marginalized communities. This means researching the companies we buy from and making informed choices about where we invest our money.

Boycotts: Hitting Them Where It Hurts

Boycotts are a direct form of protest that has a long and storied history. When consumers refuse to support companies that fund harmful political agendas, they create financial pressure that forces those companies to reconsider their actions. Boycotts are effective because they make the connection between money and power explicit. When enough people refuse to support a company, it is forced to reconsider its behavior, especially when the boycott leads to a significant drop in sales.

Boycotts are not new to the fight for justice. From the Montgomery Bus Boycott during the Civil Rights Movement to the boycott of grapes and lettuce by farm workers in California in the 1970s, boycotts have been used to challenge oppressive economic systems and force change. In each case, the goal was to hit the oppressor where it hurt most, their profits. The same strategy can be applied to corporations that fund the far-right agenda.

Take, for example, the role of Amazon in funding far-right causes. Amazon, one of the largest and most influential corporations in the world, has made significant political contributions to conservative PACs and far-right causes. By choosing to divest from Amazon, either through boycotts of their products or by pressuring companies and institutions that rely on Amazon services to stop supporting them, we can create a powerful financial incentive for Amazon to change its behavior. Other companies like Coca-Cola, Home Depot, and Disney also support conservative political candidates and causes. Boycotting these companies is a strategic way to hit the far-right where it matters, through the power of the consumer dollar.

The Power of Collective Action: Overcoming Corporate Immunity

While boycotts and divestment are powerful tools, they are not always sufficient on their own. The far-right's corporate allies are deeply entrenched in the political system, with access to significant resources and legal protections that allow them to continue their harmful activities with little consequence. That's why collective action is essential. The 4B Movement must work together to create coordinated campaigns that target corporate funding of far-right causes and ensure that these companies are held accountable.

Organizing these collective actions requires public awareness, coordination, and strategy. Activists can create awareness through social media, grassroots organizing, and public demonstrations that highlight the ways in which corporations are funding the far-right agenda. It's important to build coalitions with labor unions, environmental groups, racial justice organizations, and others who are also impacted by corporate greed and far-right politics. By working together, we can amplify our collective power and create a broader movement that holds corporations accountable for their political influence.

When consumers, activists, and investors unite in their opposition to corporations that fund the far-right, they send a clear message: these companies are not above accountability. They cannot continue to profit off political oppression without consequences. By hitting them where it hurts, through boycotts, divestment, and collective action, we can starve the corporations that sustain the far-right's agenda and build a more just and equitable economic system.

The strategy of targeting corporate power through divestment and boycotts is not just about disrupting individual companies, it is about dismantling the economic structures that sustain the far-right's agenda. The far-right's financial backbone isn't just a few bad actors; it is a web of interconnected industries, financial institutions, and mega-corporations that fund and perpetuate a system of oppression. The success of divestment and boycotts as tactics in the 4B Movement relies on understanding that these corporations and entities don't just benefit financially from policies, they actively use their wealth to maintain power over political structures, push legislation, and alter the course of social policy. To starve their influence, we must challenge their financial roots at every level, from the individual consumer to the institutional investor.

Real-World Case Studies: When Boycotts and Divestment Worked

History provides powerful examples of how boycotts and divestment campaigns have effectively challenged entrenched corporate power. One of the most prominent examples is the global boycott of companies that did business with apartheid South Africa in the 1980s. As the apartheid regime clung to power, activists around the world, supported by governments, labor unions, and civil society organizations, mounted a concerted effort to divest from companies operating in South Africa. This global movement included universities, pension funds, religious institutions, and major corporations, all of whom pulled investments out of South Africa in a bid to undermine the apartheid regime.

The divestment campaign succeeded because it placed economic pressure on South African businesses and global corporations that continued to profit from apartheid. It also demonstrated how powerful the coordinated actions of individuals, institutions, and activists could be when directed at corporate complicity in systemic injustice. While apartheid wasn't dismantled overnight, the divestment campaign, alongside internal and international pressure, helped to isolate the apartheid regime economically and politically, contributing to its eventual downfall.

The divestment from fossil fuels is another example of how targeting corporations at their financial core can shift power. The fossil fuel divestment movement, led by climate activists, has pressured universities, public institutions, and large investors to divest from fossil fuel companies in an effort to combat climate change. Over the last decade, divestment campaigns have led to billions of dollars being pulled from oil, gas, and coal companies. Financial institutions like the Rockefeller Brothers Fund, the Norwegian Sovereign Wealth Fund, and even cities like New York have pledged to divest from fossil fuels, citing both financial risks and ethical considerations surrounding the environmental impact of these industries.

In both cases, divestment didn't just hit companies where it hurt, they also sent a clear signal to the political establishment. By making it economically unfeasible for major institutions to continue supporting systems of oppression, divestment campaigns created a path toward broader societal change. These campaigns didn't just target individual companies, they targeted the entire industry, making it harder for companies to operate in an environment that was hostile to their profits.

By taking a page from these successful campaigns, the 4B Movement can apply the same tactics to corporations funding far-right agendas, starting by identifying their financial ties to right-wing political movements and using collective action to financially isolate them.

The Financial Backbone of the Far-Right

To effectively starve the corporations that fund the far-right, we must first understand the complex relationships between money and politics. The far-right agenda is not just pushed by politicians, it is backed by powerful economic forces that rely on the perpetuation of inequality, deregulation, and the concentration of wealth. These corporations are not simply donating to candidates, they are actively funding think tanks, PACs, and lobbying groups that drive the political discourse toward policies that protect their financial interests.

For example, Koch Industries, one of the largest privately held companies in the world, has been a major financier of libertarian and conservative causes for decades. The Koch family has poured billions into efforts to roll back environmental protections, resist the implementation of labor rights, and eliminate corporate taxes. Their political arm, Americans for Prosperity, was instrumental in shaping the Tea Party movement and pushing anti-tax, anti-regulation agendas at both the state and federal levels. Koch Industries is far from the only company doing this, but it serves as a clear example of how economic interests fuel political movements.

Other corporations, particularly in the energy and pharmaceutical industries, have also been key players in supporting far-right movements. ExxonMobil, for instance, has not only funded climate change denial campaigns but also supported political candidates and PACs that actively work to dismantle regulations on emissions, the environment, and renewable energy. Companies like Amazon, despite their progressive public image, have also come under scrutiny for their lobbying efforts in favor of conservative policies, particularly regarding workers' rights and unionization efforts.

The goal of these corporations is clear: they want to preserve a system in which they control the resources, the economy, and the political decision-making process. Their agenda is one of maintaining power and ensuring that wealth is concentrated at the top. This creates a dangerous feedback loop: these corporations fund far-right politicians, who, in turn, pass laws that benefit these corporations at the expense of the broader population. The more these corporations fund right-wing movements, the more power they accumulate, creating a cycle of political and economic dominance.

Divestment as a Direct Attack on Corporate Power

Divestment is a direct way to disrupt this cycle of corporate power. By strategically withdrawing investments from companies that fund far-right agendas, we reduce their financial resources and weaken their political influence. This process involves both large-scale institutional divestment (e.g., universities, pension funds, governments) as well as individual action. Whether it's refusing to invest in certain companies through retirement funds or choosing not to buy products from companies known for their financial support of harmful political causes, every action contributes to the broader goal of cutting off their financial lifeblood.

The impact of divestment can be profound. As more organizations and institutions pledge to divest from companies funding far-right movements, it increases the financial pressure on these corporations. These divestment campaigns force companies to respond publicly to criticism and may even push them to reconsider their political alliances. Over time, divesting from these corporations can lead to a broader shift in the way companies and financial institutions operate. They will be less likely to engage in activities that harm people or the environment if doing so causes a measurable financial loss.

Another strategy for divestment involves moving capital toward socially responsible investment (SRI) and environmental, social, and governance (ESG) funds. By supporting companies that prioritize human rights, environmental sustainability, and ethical practices, we send a clear message that the financial world cannot ignore consumers and investors demand ethical action. Supporting companies that align with progressive values not only divests from the harmful corporations propping up far-right movements, but it also strengthens the financial power of companies that prioritize social responsibility.

Boycotts: A Practical Guide for Direct Action

Boycotts have long been a powerful tool for social movements, providing a direct way for individuals to withdraw their financial support from corporations that engage in harmful practices. In the 4B Movement, boycotts are a strategic weapon for targeting the corporations that fund far-right political agendas. By mobilizing consumers, workers, and investors to boycott companies that support theocratic fascism, we can create significant pressure on these corporations, forcing them to reconsider their positions.

Boycotting doesn't just mean refusing to purchase a company's products, it means refusing to support any part of their business model that contributes to the far-right's agenda. This includes boycotting their stores, cutting ties with their services, and challenging institutions that invest in them. One of the most powerful aspects of boycotts is their ability to raise public awareness. When a major company is publicly boycotted, it forces the company to address the issue, often resulting in media coverage, public debate, and, sometimes, changes in corporate behavior.

Take, for instance, the boycott of Chick-fil-A, which became a flashpoint for discussions on corporate involvement in far-right politics. In 2012, it was revealed that the company's executives had made significant donations to anti-LGBTQ+ organizations, leading to a nationwide boycott. While the boycott did not immediately shut down Chick-fil-A's business, it forced the company to reassess its public image and its association with far-right causes. The boycott, combined with protests, created a national conversation about the role of corporations in supporting political movements, forcing companies like Chick-fil-A to weigh the potential backlash from their financial support of harmful ideologies.

In the same vein, the 4B Movement can target corporations that fund far-right political candidates and PACs, applying the pressure of consumer boycotts to weaken their influence. Companies like

Walmart, which have supported conservative causes and politicians, are prime targets for such action. By boycotting their stores, refusing to purchase their products, and demanding that other businesses and organizations stop doing business with them, we can create financial pressure that forces them to reconsider their support for anti-humanitarian policies.

A successful boycott is not just about withdrawing money, it's about making that withdrawal meaningful. It's about organizing, spreading the word, and creating a unified front that makes it impossible for these companies to ignore the impact of their actions. Boycotts are most effective when they are part of a broader movement that includes divestment, legal action, and public advocacy. Together, these actions create a unified challenge to the corporate interests that fund far-right movements, weakening their financial grip and exposing the ways they use their wealth to influence politics.

Top Consumer Product Donors to the GOP

ExxonMobil	CVS Health	Costco
Walmart	Johnson & Johnson	Sam's Club
Home Depot	Kroger	BJ's Wholesale
Lockheed Martin	Apple	Club
Boeing	McDonald's	Lowe's Home
Comcast	Facebook (Meta)	Improvement
AT&T	Amazon	Ace Hardware
Coca-Cola	Nike	True Value
Chevron	General Electric	Menards
Eli Lilly	Rite Aid	Sears
Bank of America	Marriott	J.C. Penney
Wells Fargo	International	Macy's
Target	Citibank	Nordstrom
PepsiCo	CVS Pharmacy	Kohl's
Visa	Walgreens	Dillard's
Procter & Gamble	Kroger	Belk
General Motors	Safeway	Saks Fifth Avenue
Lowe's	Albertsons	Pfizer

Unions and Labor Strikes

Unions and labor strikes have long been powerful tools for workers to demand better working conditions, higher wages, and more equitable treatment from employers. As direct action, these tactics challenge the power structures that exploit labor for profit. The essence of labor strikes is rooted in collective action: workers withholding their labor to disrupt business operations, forcing employers to the bargaining table. Strikes aren't just symbolic protests, they are economic disruptions that can compel change in ways that other forms of protest often cannot. Unions, as collective organizations of workers, are the backbone of labor strikes. They provide the organizational structure, the legal support, and the collective bargaining power that enable workers to stand united in the face of corporate interests. Throughout history, unions have fought for many of the rights workers enjoy today, including the eight-hour workday, minimum wage laws, and safe working conditions. Their power lies in the ability to mobilize large groups of workers and challenge the power of employers.

Strikes, as a form of direct action, force employers to feel the consequences of their actions. When workers walk off the job, they create a vacuum in productivity that can cost companies millions of dollars. This financial pressure is often what drives employers to make concessions, whether that's in the form of higher wages, improved benefits, or better working conditions. Strikes often draw attention to the inequities workers face, galvanizing public support and putting pressure on policymakers to act. In recent years, labor strikes have made a resurgence, with workers in fast food, retail, and other service industries organizing to demand fair pay and better working conditions. Teachers, healthcare workers, and tech employees have also engaged in strikes, demonstrating that labor action is not limited to traditional blue-collar industries. The power of unions and strikes is clear: they force corporations to reckon with the realities of labor exploitation and challenge the systems that allow it to persist. By using strikes as a form of direct action, workers are not just fighting for their rights, they are fighting for a fairer, more just society.

Chapter 8~BOYCOTT
Buying Into Liberation

In the fight for liberation, the economic systems we support and participate in are just as important as the political movements we join. For too long, the vast majority of economic power has been concentrated in the hands of a few, and these corporations have consistently fueled oppression, inequality, and exploitation. From multinational giants that fund the far-right agenda to industries that profit off the systemic disenfranchisement of marginalized communities, our consumer choices have often sustained the very structures of power we seek to dismantle. As we rise up against these systems, we must begin to look inward and ask ourselves how we can support the revolution with every dollar we spend, every product we buy, and every service we seek. One of the most powerful ways to do this is by creating networks of women-owned, progressive-friendly businesses that actively work to build parallel economies that reject the systems of oppression.

For centuries, the economic landscape has been dominated by men, especially white men, who have controlled the capital, labor, and resources that have driven most industries. Women, particularly women of color, have been systematically excluded from wealth-building opportunities and denied access to the networks and resources that would enable them to build businesses of their own. In response, we must not only break the chains of this exclusion but also build alternatives that actively uplift those who have been pushed to the margins of the economy. The future of liberation lies in creating a network of businesses that center the needs and desires of women, people of color, the LGBTQ+ community, and other historically marginalized groups. These businesses should not only be places of economic exchange but also sites of social change, where values of justice, equity, and solidarity are embedded in every transaction.

The concept of building a parallel economy is not new. Throughout history, marginalized communities have created their own economic systems in response to being shut out of mainstream markets. During the Civil Rights Movement, African Americans built networks of businesses, churches, and social organizations that allowed them to function in a world that denied them basic rights and economic opportunities. The Black Wall Street in Tulsa, Oklahoma, before its violent destruction by white supremacists, is perhaps the most famous example of a thriving, self-sustaining Black community that existed outside the economic structures of the mainstream. Similarly, Indigenous communities have long created their own systems of trade and support, often operating outside of colonial economic systems that sought to exploit their land and labor. These examples demonstrate the power of parallel economies in creating resilient, self-sufficient communities that prioritize the well-being of their members over corporate profit.

Today, the idea of parallel economies is more critical than ever. In a world where the corporate elite continues to consolidate power, draining the wealth of working people and funneling it into political and social systems that maintain inequality, building alternative economic structures is a necessary act of resistance. This means creating spaces for women-owned businesses, progressive cooperatives, and organizations that prioritize community over profit. These businesses must not only offer goods and services that meet the needs of the people but must also do so in a way that challenges the status quo. The goal is to create businesses that are sustainable, just, and equitable, businesses that support labor rights, protect the environment, and contribute to a society that values human life over capital.

One of the primary challenges in building these businesses is access to capital. For women and people of color, securing the financial resources to start and sustain a business has historically been an uphill battle. Women entrepreneurs, especially those from marginalized backgrounds, are often excluded from the networks of investors and venture capitalists that fund the majority of new businesses. This exclusion is not just a matter of economics, it is a reflection of a broader systemic issue of oppression, where the very resources necessary for self-determination are denied to those who have historically been oppressed. To build a parallel economy, we must create mechanisms for women and marginalized communities to access the capital they need to start and grow businesses. This could involve creating alternative lending systems, like community-based lending circles or co-op funding models, where people invest in each other's businesses rather than relying on traditional banks that are deeply entangled with corporate and political power.

In parallel to this, it is crucial to support women-owned businesses by making intentional consumer choices. Every dollar spent is a vote for the kind of world we want to live in. When we buy from companies that align with our values, businesses that are worker-owned, support fair wages, and use their profits to benefit communities, we are rejecting the consumerist culture that drives much of the oppression in our society. Whether it's supporting local, sustainable businesses or finding brands that prioritize ethical practices, our collective purchasing power can have a massive impact. By creating demand for businesses that value social justice, environmental sustainability, and economic equity, we can begin to reshape the economy from the ground up. This shift isn't just about individual actions, it's about building a culture of resistance that says we won't continue to support businesses that exploit workers, harm the environment, or prop up unjust systems.

Of course, building a parallel economy isn't easy. The corporate power structure is deeply entrenched, and the forces that sustain it, through lobbying, media influence, and the consolidation of wealth, are vast and formidable. Yet, there is growing recognition of the need to build alternatives. People are tired of being complicit in systems that harm the most vulnerable, and they are actively seeking out ways to invest their time, money, and energy into something better. From small, local businesses to large, progressive cooperatives, the rise of women-led, community-centered economic enterprises offers a hopeful vision of what a more just and equitable world could look like. In these businesses, people can find products, services, and experiences that align with their values, businesses that are not just out to make a profit, but to make a difference.

The rise of progressive women-owned businesses is not just about creating an alternative to the corporate world, it is about rethinking the entire purpose of business itself. In a capitalist society driven by the profit motive, businesses often operate with one primary goal: to maximize returns for shareholders. This model leads to the exploitation of workers, the degradation of the environment, and the concentration of wealth in the hands of a few. But women-led businesses can offer a different vision. These businesses can prioritize people over profit, community over consumption, and justice over exploitation. They can be sites of social change that offer a more humane alternative to the corporate world. By investing in businesses that prioritize the well-being of workers, the community, and the environment, we begin to create the foundation for an economy that works for all people.

Creating networks of women-owned, progressive-friendly businesses is also about building solidarity and collective power. The success of one business in this network is tied to the success of others. These businesses can support each other through collaborative efforts, whether it's sharing resources, engaging in joint marketing campaigns, or advocating for common political goals. In a world where the corporate elite work together to maintain their power, it's essential that those of us fighting for liberation work together in the same way. By creating networks of support, these businesses can create a foundation for a broader movement that challenges the corporate hegemony and builds a more just and sustainable economy.

As we build these alternative networks, we must also be mindful of the need to confront the corporate power structures that continue to exploit workers, communities, and the environment. While creating alternative economies is important, it is also essential to continue fighting the systems of oppression that perpetuate inequality. This means challenging the corporations that fund theocratic fascism, fighting for labor rights, and advocating for policies that promote economic justice. Building parallel economies is not a substitute for political action, it is a complement to it. It is a way to create the economic power necessary to back up our demands for political change.

Ultimately, buying into liberation means recognizing that our economic choices are political choices. When we choose to support businesses that align with our values, we are engaging in a form of resistance that challenges the systems of power that perpetuate injustice. By investing in women-owned, progressive-friendly businesses, we begin to build an economy that is rooted in justice, equity, and solidarity. This is not just an economic strategy, it is a revolutionary act that seeks to reimagine the world we live in and create the conditions for true liberation.

As we continue to build these networks of women-owned, progressive-friendly businesses, we must also recognize that the power of consumerism extends far beyond just buying from companies with aligned values. The real work of creating parallel economies requires a complete shift in how we view economic transactions and the roles they play in perpetuating or dismantling oppression. To fully understand the scope of this shift, we need to break down the structure of the existing economy and build alternatives that do not rely on exploitation, inequality, and environmental degradation. This is a process that involves creating new economic systems that prioritize justice, equality, sustainability, and community, and that are driven by the needs of marginalized groups rather than the profit motives of corporations.

For far too long, our consumer habits have been shaped by a global capitalist system that thrives on exploitation. The vast majority of corporations, regardless of whether they are in the tech, retail, energy, or food sectors, operate with one central goal: to maximize profit at all costs. This means that they exploit labor, destroy the environment, and perpetuate economic systems that concentrate wealth and power in the hands of the few. They rely on cheap labor, often from communities of color, migrant workers, and women, to maintain their margins. These corporations benefit from policies that undermine workers' rights, destroy labor unions, and give them the ability to influence political systems in their favor. We see this daily through lobbyist groups, political donations, and corporate PACs that work to shape legislation in ways that benefit the wealthiest while harming the rest of society.

In light of this, building a parallel economy means actively rejecting this system and creating something new, something that not only resists exploitation but offers an alternative economic structure. By supporting women-owned businesses and cooperative enterprises, we begin to build a network that rejects corporate greed in favor of solidarity and mutual benefit. But for these new economies to flourish, we must take steps to ensure they are not only viable but sustainable in the long term.

A central element of these alternative economies is the establishment of worker cooperatives, businesses that are owned and run by the people who work for them. These cooperatives prioritize worker welfare over profit maximization and distribute earnings equitably among their members. The beauty of worker cooperatives lies in their ability to redistribute power and wealth within communities. Unlike traditional businesses, where decisions are made by a small group of executives with little regard for the well-being of workers, worker cooperatives are democratic organizations where every worker has an equal say in how the business is run. This means that wages, working conditions, and business practices are decided collectively, and profits are shared equitably. In the context of building a parallel economy, cooperatives serve as models of economic democracy, providing an alternative to the exploitative practices of corporate-owned businesses.

There are already numerous examples of worker cooperatives flourishing in various industries, proving that this model works. The Cooperative Home Care Associates (CHCA) in New York is a prime example. As one of the largest worker cooperatives in the U.S., CHCA provides home health care services to vulnerable populations while offering their workers fair wages, benefits, and a democratic voice in their workplace. This cooperative has demonstrated that businesses can provide essential services, create good-paying jobs, and remain economically viable, all while upholding values of social justice. Similarly, the Mondragón Corporation in the Basque Country of Spain has grown into one of the world's largest and most successful cooperatives, with more than 80,000 workers across hundreds of businesses in various sectors, from manufacturing to retail. These examples show that alternative economic models not only resist the exploitation seen in traditional capitalist structures but also provide better working conditions, equitable pay, and more stable communities.

While worker cooperatives represent a powerful alternative, creating a parallel economy also requires addressing the broader systems of wealth and power that reinforce corporate dominance. One of the most critical aspects of this process is addressing the financial infrastructure that supports corporate power. Traditional financial institutions like banks, hedge funds, and venture capital firms are complicit in the perpetuation of inequality. They invest heavily in industries that harm the environment, exploit workers, and perpetuate economic injustice. To build a truly parallel economy, we must shift our financial resources away from these institutions and direct them toward community-based banks, credit unions, and alternative lending networks that prioritize social impact over profit.

One such example is the community development financial institution (CDFI), which is designed to provide financial services to communities that are underserved by traditional banks. CDFIs focus on providing loans to small businesses, affordable housing projects, and community initiatives in low-income areas, especially those that are predominantly Black, Indigenous, and people of color. These financial institutions operate on a much smaller scale than corporate banks, but they have been successful in creating positive social change by channeling capital into communities that are often overlooked by larger financial institutions. Supporting CDFIs and other socially responsible financial institutions is one way to ensure that our money is being used to build a more just and equitable economy.

Building a parallel economy also means investing in community infrastructure that supports social and environmental well-being. This includes supporting local farmers, artisans, and independent businesses that are committed to ethical practices and environmental sustainability. By buying from these businesses, we are investing in a local economy that serves the needs of people rather than corporations. In this way, we begin to create economies that operate on a human scale, where relationships between producers and consumers are rooted in fairness and cooperation rather than exploitation and profit maximization.

Another critical element of building a parallel economy is ensuring that it is inclusive and accessible to all people, especially those who have been historically excluded from economic power. This means focusing on creating economic opportunities for women, people of color, LGBTQ+ individuals, and other marginalized communities. It also means addressing the systemic barriers that prevent these groups from accessing capital, resources, and networks that are necessary to start and grow businesses. In many ways, the parallel economy must work to undo the structural inequalities that have been perpetuated by traditional capitalism. This includes advocating for policies that support paid family leave, universal healthcare, affordable childcare, and affordable housing, all of which are essential for enabling marginalized communities to thrive economically.

Moreover, creating a parallel economy requires a cultural shift. It requires challenging the pervasive notion that success is defined by individual wealth accumulation and instead promoting the idea that collective well-being is the true measure of success. In this new economy, we prioritize mutual aid, cooperation, and collective action over competition and self-interest. This cultural shift can be seen in the growing popularity of worker cooperatives, ethical consumerism, and grassroots movements that prioritize collective welfare. By supporting businesses and organizations that reflect these values, we are contributing to a larger cultural shift away from individualism and toward a more inclusive, just society.

This is also a moment to reconsider what we consume. The choices we make as consumers hold incredible power. Every time we buy something, we are casting a vote for the type of world we want to live in. Instead of supporting multinational corporations that extract resources, exploit labor, and fund harmful political movements, we can choose to support businesses that operate with integrity and a commitment to justice. This can mean choosing to buy from local artisans, choosing to invest in fair-trade products, or choosing to support businesses that have a track record of treating their workers well and paying them fair wages. It's not always easy to make these choices, especially when they come with a higher price tag or more inconvenience, but the impact of our choices can be profound. If millions of consumers began redirecting their spending to businesses that align with their values, it could have a massive impact on the way the economy functions.

The creation of a parallel economy is a long-term project, one that requires sustained effort and dedication. But the vision is clear: an economy that prioritizes human dignity, environmental sustainability, and social justice over corporate greed. Building this economy requires the active participation of everyone who believes in a more just, equitable, and sustainable world. It is a challenge, but it is also an opportunity to create a new economic system that serves the needs of all people, rather than the few.

20 Humane Policies to Fight For

1.   Universal Healthcare

Advocating for a single-payer or universal healthcare system ensures that all individuals, regardless of income or status, have access to necessary medical care. This would reduce healthcare disparities, improve overall public health, and eliminate the profit-driven motives of private healthcare corporations.

2.   Living Wage Legislation

A living wage law would require companies to pay workers enough to meet basic living expenses, ensuring that no one working full-time lives in poverty. This policy is critical in closing income inequality and addressing wage stagnation, especially for workers in low-wage industries.

3.   Paid Family and Medical Leave

Providing paid leave for workers who need to care for a newborn, family member, or recover from an illness promotes better work-life balance, strengthens family bonds, and ensures that workers aren't forced to choose between their health or their livelihood.

4.   Green New Deal

A comprehensive climate policy that focuses on transitioning to renewable energy, creating green jobs, and addressing environmental justice for communities that have been disproportionately harmed by pollution. This policy aims to mitigate climate change while promoting economic equality and sustainability.

5.   Affordable Housing Initiatives

Advocating for the construction of affordable housing and rent control policies can help address homelessness, reduce housing insecurity, and ensure everyone has access to safe, stable living conditions. Housing should be considered a human right, not a commodity.

6.   Criminal Justice Reform

Policies aimed at ending mass incarceration, eliminating private prisons, reforming sentencing laws, and decriminalizing non-violent offenses will help reduce the racial disparities in the criminal justice system and prioritize rehabilitation over punishment.

7.   Universal Basic Income (UBI)

A UBI policy would provide all individuals with a guaranteed income to cover basic needs, regardless of employment status. This policy addresses poverty, income inequality, and provides financial security, especially in a rapidly changing labor market due to automation.

8.	Free College Education and Student Debt Forgiveness
Making college education free for all and forgiving existing student loan debt would provide equitable access to education, reduce the financial burdens on young people, and increase opportunities for economic mobility.

9.	LGBTQ+ Rights Protection
Strong anti-discrimination policies to protect LGBTQ+ individuals in all areas of life, including employment, housing, healthcare, and public accommodations, are crucial in ensuring equality and fighting systemic discrimination.

10.	Racial Justice and Reparations
Policies aimed at addressing the historical injustices and systemic discrimination faced by Black and Indigenous people, including reparations programs, investments in education, healthcare, and community infrastructure for historically marginalized communities.

11.	Voting Rights Protection
Strengthening voting rights, eliminating voter suppression tactics, and expanding access to the ballot box will ensure that all citizens, particularly marginalized groups, can participate in the democratic process without barriers.

12.	Gun Control Legislation
Stricter gun control laws, including universal background checks, banning assault weapons, and enacting mandatory gun buybacks, would help reduce gun violence, mass shootings, and improve public safety.

13.	Worker's Rights Protection
Policies that strengthen labor unions, protect workers from exploitation, and ensure safe and fair working conditions are essential to empowering the workforce and ensuring that workers have a collective voice in the workplace.

14.	Corporate Tax Reform
Advocating for higher taxes on corporations and the wealthiest individuals to fund social programs, reduce income inequality, and ensure that companies pay their fair share of taxes to the government rather than relying on tax loopholes and offshore accounts.

15.	Comprehensive Immigration Reform
Policies that protect immigrant rights, provide pathways to citizenship, and ensure fair treatment for undocumented individuals will promote equality, economic integration, and protect vulnerable communities from exploitation and abuse.

16.	Climate Justice and Environmental Protection
This policy would focus on addressing environmental injustices
disproportionately affecting low-income and marginalized
communities. It includes strengthening environmental protections,
holding corporations accountable for pollution, and ensuring
equitable access to clean air, water, and green spaces. It would also
involve investment in sustainable infrastructure, renewable energy,
and climate resilience for vulnerable communities, helping to mitigate
the effects of climate change while ensuring a just transition to a green
economy.
17.	Universal Childcare and Early Education
This policy would ensure access to affordable, high-quality childcare
and early childhood education for all families. It would reduce the
financial burden on working parents, support child development, and
provide equal educational opportunities from a young age, helping to
close the achievement gap and promote long-term societal equity.
18.	End to Corporate Lobbying and Political Influence
Advocate for policies that restrict corporate lobbying and the
influence of money in politics. This would include campaign finance
reforms, transparency in political donations, and limits on the
revolving door between government and corporate interests.
Reducing corporate influence in politics ensures that legislation serves
the needs of the people rather than the profit motives of big business.
19.	Mental Health Access and Support
Strengthening access to mental health care through expanded
services, reduced stigma, and better insurance coverage would address
the growing mental health crisis. This policy would include support
for mental health in schools, workplaces, and communities, ensuring
that everyone has access to the care they need to thrive, and
destigmatizing mental health challenges.
20.	Affordable and Clean Energy Access
Expanding access to affordable, clean energy sources such as solar,
wind, and geothermal energy is essential to combating climate change
and ensuring energy security for all. This policy would focus on
incentivizing renewable energy use in low-income communities,
providing subsidies for clean energy infrastructure, and transitioning
away from fossil fuels to create a sustainable, equitable energy future.

Chapter 9~BOYCOTT
Callout Culture Beyond Cancel Culture

In the digital age, callout culture has taken on a life of its own. Social media has given individuals and groups unprecedented power to call out bad behavior, whether it's racism, sexism, corporate greed, or political corruption. Yet, while online movements have helped raise awareness about critical issues, too often these calls for accountability remain just that, calls. Hashtags trend, conversations start, but tangible change is slow, if it happens at all. The problem lies in the fact that callouts have become performative. Social media platforms thrive on short-lived outrage, and corporate figures or public personalities frequently know how to ride out the storm. What we need is a model of callout culture that goes beyond the performative and creates lasting, structural change. This is about shifting from outrage to economic activism, creating real pressure on corporations and public figures to act with integrity, justice, and accountability.

The key to making callout culture effective lies in direct action. A callout is no longer enough if it doesn't lead to measurable consequences for the wrongdoer. Whether it's boycotting companies, withdrawing financial support, or leveraging the collective power of consumers, direct action is what makes the difference between a viral moment and real change. Companies and public figures understand one thing above all: money. The pressure we must apply must be targeted at their wallets. When we take our purchasing power away, when we use our influence to demand accountability, and when we refuse to support those who perpetuate harm, we create an economic movement that they can't ignore.

For this to work, we need to make the connections clear. Consumers must be educated about the economic power they hold and how their choices, every dollar they spend, directly influence corporate behavior. It is not enough to post a tweet with a hashtag and move on to the next issue. We must hold corporations accountable in ways that affect their bottom line. The pressure needs to be sustained, coordinated, and strategic. It's not just about calling out individuals or organizations; it's about creating the conditions where their actions become untenable and financially damaging.

The rise of economic activism in recent years has shown that collective action can create meaningful change. In 2018, for example, the #BoycottNike campaign, sparked by the company's decision to feature Colin Kaepernick in their ad campaign, quickly gained momentum. Far-right groups called for a boycott of Nike, yet, in the end, Nike saw a significant increase in sales and brand value. The company's response to the callout wasn't just to ride out the storm. Nike stood by its decision, signaling that the values of social justice, equality, and resistance mattered more than catering to a consumer base that didn't share those values. This was a turning point. Nike's success in handling the situation demonstrated that corporations could make bold political and social decisions without fearing backlash if they stood firm.

The lesson here is that corporations are increasingly aware of their consumer base's values and will, in many cases, lean into activism if it serves their long-term interests. However, for this to be genuine and sustainable, corporations must understand that they are not immune to pressure from consumers. This means shifting from performative outrage to sustained, collective efforts. It is about holding corporations accountable for their actions, whether they are paying fair wages, ensuring environmental sustainability, or taking political stances that align with justice. Simply calling out a company or a celebrity isn't enough if that callout isn't backed up by collective economic pressure that forces a response.

A key example of economic activism in recent history is the #MeToo movement and the impact it had on industries from entertainment to politics. In 2017, allegations against Hollywood mogul Harvey Weinstein sparked a global reckoning around sexual harassment and abuse. The #MeToo movement exploded across social media, leading to the downfall of numerous public figures, many of whom lost lucrative contracts, endorsements, and careers. However, the movement also demonstrated that while public accountability was crucial, the true power of the movement lay in its ability to affect industries economically. Sponsors pulled funding from companies and figures associated with abusers, and public figures were swiftly dropped from their positions or contracts. This economic consequence made it clear that individuals and corporations could not escape accountability when their actions impacted the public trust.

What made the #MeToo movement successful wasn't just the exposure of harmful behaviors but the subsequent action taken to hold abusers accountable. Boycotts, protests, and financial withdrawal from industries that protected abusers sent a strong signal that the time for turning a blind eye had passed. It wasn't enough for individuals to simply call out others on social media. The movement became a tangible force because it combined outrage with collective action that took financial power away from those who had been complicit.

This economic power is critical because corporations, by their nature, are profit-driven entities. They are motivated to preserve their revenue streams, which means any threat to their financial stability can spur change. Effective economic activism means going beyond social media campaigns to build broader coalitions that create pressure on corporations. It means calling for boycotts that are strategic and sustained. It means pulling financial support, withdrawing investments, and leveraging consumer behavior to hold corporations and public figures accountable. The stronger and more coordinated these efforts are, the more likely we are to see real, lasting changes in corporate practices and political behavior.

Another example of this is seen in the fight for fair wages and workers' rights. Companies like Amazon, Walmart, and McDonald's have faced growing calls for higher wages and better working conditions for their employees. In 2018, the Fight for $15 movement made a significant push, gaining traction and widespread public support. This movement, which advocated for a $15 minimum wage and union rights for fast food workers, utilized economic activism to apply pressure on corporations that profit from low-wage labor. The movement brought workers into the streets, into boardrooms, and into the media, demanding that these corporations pay their employees a living wage. When people boycott businesses, demand better labor laws, or support unionization efforts, they demonstrate that corporate profits cannot come at the expense of workers' rights.

Fast-food chains like McDonald's and fast retail companies like Walmart have felt the pressure from these movements. The same has been true for major corporations that have relied on outsourced, low-wage labor to boost their margins. Boycotts and protests around the Fight for $15 have forced companies like McDonald's to raise wages at some of their locations and to offer better benefits for employees. While the movement has faced setbacks, the pressure placed on companies and policymakers to address the realities of low-wage work is undeniable. The impact of economic activism here is clear: when consumers and workers unite to demand better, the financial incentives for corporations shift, and change becomes possible.

The effectiveness of this kind of economic activism rests on the collective ability of communities to hold companies accountable, not just on individual actions. If we want callout culture to work, it has to be tied to a movement that integrates sustained financial pressure with direct action. It's not enough to post a hashtag and wait for change to happen on its own. We must take the lessons of recent history, whether it's the economic boycotts surrounding #MeToo or the Fight for $15, and create movements that apply pressure where it counts: in the boardroom, on Wall Street, and in the pockets of those who perpetuate harm.

When we look at companies like Nike, McDonald's, and Amazon, they are not just corporate entities, they are reflections of a larger system that prioritizes profit over people. The goal of economic activism is to flip this script. We must reject the narrative that business as usual can continue without consequence. Consumers, workers, and activists have the power to reshape the economy by directing resources to businesses that support justice, equality, and sustainability, while withdrawing support from those that fund oppression, exploitation, and environmental destruction. Economic activism isn't just about calling out bad actors, it's about changing the system that allows them to thrive. When we build networks of support around businesses that are progressive, ethical, and community-centered, we lay the foundation for a more just and equitable future.

This is the power of callout culture that actually works. It moves from online outrage to real-world, tangible change. It's about holding corporations and individuals accountable in ways that force them to reckon with their actions and make lasting changes. By demanding change, applying economic pressure, and organizing in solidarity, we make it clear that the age of unchecked corporate power is over. We are the consumers, we are the workers, and we are the change-makers.

Diving Deeper

In the second part of this exploration into effective callout culture, we dive deeper into the practicalities of economic activism and its transformative potential. While part one illuminated the principles behind creating real change, shifting from performative outrage to meaningful pressure, it's now time to examine the mechanics of building movements that can make corporations, public figures, and political systems accountable. The strategies we employ must be as sophisticated as the systems we are fighting, and economic activism provides the blueprint for this kind of sustained, strategic pressure.

The first step in creating economic activism that works is building a coalition of people committed to using their collective financial power as a force for social change. In this context, economic power is not just about individual consumer choices, but rather a unified, collective action that targets corporations, industries, and financial institutions that perpetuate inequality, environmental degradation, and exploitation. As individuals, we may feel small in comparison to the corporate behemoths we're up against, but when we combine forces, our economic power becomes undeniable. The key to a successful movement is not just identifying a problem, but organizing people to actively participate in a campaign that applies economic pressure in a strategic, coordinated way.

One of the most effective ways to build collective economic power is by organizing boycotts that directly target corporations or industries that are complicit in perpetuating harm. A successful boycott is not simply about choosing not to buy from a company. It is about making the boycott large enough and sustained long enough that the company feels the economic consequences. The larger the number of people who commit to the boycott, the more likely it is that the company will be forced to act. The power of economic pressure lies in the ability to drain a corporation's resources, forcing them to acknowledge that their consumer base and employees will not stand for harmful practices.

To execute an effective boycott, strategic planning and education are key. Activists need to identify the corporations or industries that are most responsible for harmful actions, whether it's contributing to climate change, perpetuating gender or racial inequality, or supporting political agendas that harm marginalized groups. Once targets are identified, the next step is organizing a large base of consumers, workers, and community members who are willing to take action. This involves not only raising awareness but also providing clear alternatives. Consumers should be empowered to know which businesses align with their values, and what the impact of their spending choices could be. For example, if a corporation has been exposed for exploiting workers or funding political movements that harm LGBTQ+ rights, providing consumers with alternatives, such as fair-trade or worker-owned businesses, can guide them in making more ethical choices.

Boycotts, however, must not be short-lived. A one-day or one-week boycott is rarely enough to pressure corporations into taking real action. For sustained economic activism, boycotts must be part of an ongoing campaign, with clear messaging that outlines why the boycott is taking place and what demands the group is making. This can include petitions, direct actions like pickets or protests, social media campaigns, and even direct negotiations with the company. The longer the boycott lasts, the more likely it is that the corporation will feel the financial impact. Often, this sustained pressure leads companies to re-evaluate their policies or actions to protect their public image and avoid further economic harm.

Take, for instance, the 2017 boycott of Equinox and SoulCycle, which was sparked by the revelation that the companies' co-owner, Stephen Ross, was hosting a fundraiser for President Donald Trump. Many customers, particularly from the progressive community, felt compelled to take action, given Ross's ties to an administration that was hostile to issues like LGBTQ+ rights, environmental protections, and women's rights. The boycott was a powerful statement from consumers who refused to support a business that supported a leader who was openly against their values. Though it didn't immediately force Ross to divest from his political affiliations, it sent a strong message that people are willing to take their business elsewhere when corporations openly support harmful political causes.

Beyond boycotts, divestment has proven to be another effective tool in economic activism. Divesting from companies, industries, or financial institutions that uphold oppressive systems not only reduces the power of those entities but also directs resources to businesses that align with justice, sustainability, and equality. The practice of divestment has been used successfully by social movements, particularly in the fight against apartheid in South Africa and more recently in the fossil fuel divestment movement. By redirecting financial support away from industries that profit from harm, divestment campaigns send a message to corporations and investors: if you support oppressive systems, you will face a loss of support from the people who can vote with their dollars.

In the case of fossil fuel divestment, activists have pressured universities, pension funds, and even entire cities to pull investments from fossil fuel companies, thus weakening their financial power. This has had a significant impact on companies like ExxonMobil, Chevron, and Shell, forcing them to engage with the growing movement toward renewable energy and sustainable business practices. The divestment movement shows the incredible power of redirecting resources away from harmful industries and towards businesses that prioritize social good, environmental sustainability, and ethical labor practices.

But the divestment movement isn't just limited to environmental concerns. The same principles can be applied to industries that profit from human rights violations, like the prison-industrial complex, private healthcare, or the weapons manufacturing industry. When people and institutions divest from companies that profit from oppression, they force those corporations to reckon with the fact that their business practices are no longer supported by a significant portion of the population. Divestment campaigns, when effectively organized, are one of the most powerful tools in an economic activist's arsenal.

One notable success story in recent years is the growing movement to boycott and divest from big tech companies like Facebook (Meta), Google, and Amazon. These corporations have faced increased scrutiny for their role in perpetuating harmful data practices, spreading misinformation, contributing to environmental destruction, and undermining democratic processes. The backlash against Facebook, in particular, has been significant, with consumers and advertisers pulling their support from the platform due to its role in enabling hate speech, political polarization, and election interference. The rise of alternative social media platforms that prioritize user privacy and ethical practices, such as Mastodon and Signal, shows that there is a growing demand for businesses that align with social and political values that prioritize human dignity over corporate profit.

Another crucial aspect of economic activism is the role of worker solidarity and collective bargaining in driving corporate change. While boycotts and divestment campaigns focus on shifting consumer and investor behavior, worker-driven movements are essential in demanding corporate accountability. Unions and labor strikes have long been a powerful tool in securing better wages, safer working conditions, and benefits for workers. When workers organize to collectively demand better treatment, they apply direct pressure on companies to change their policies and practices. This form of economic activism is particularly effective because it disrupts business operations directly, forcing companies to negotiate with workers in good faith to avoid economic losses.

The recent wave of unionization efforts, particularly in the tech industry (such as with Amazon and Google workers), has highlighted the growing power of workers to challenge the oppressive practices of their employers. Workers in these industries are organizing around issues like fair wages, job security, and corporate responsibility in areas like privacy and ethics. These movements not only challenge the status quo within companies but also send a broader message to other corporations that workers are no longer willing to be exploited for corporate gain. This shift in power from corporate executives to workers is a fundamental part of building an economy that works for the many, not just the few.

Corporate accountability can also be achieved through regulatory reforms that require companies to be more transparent about their operations, labor practices, environmental impact, and political donations. While pressure from consumers and workers can drive some immediate changes, long-term systemic change requires policies that regulate corporate behavior. Advocating for policies that enforce stricter labor protections, corporate transparency, and environmental regulations ensures that companies cannot operate without regard for their social and environmental impact. These reforms not only help to curb corporate malfeasance but also provide a clearer path for consumers, workers, and activists to hold companies accountable.

In the end, effective economic activism requires both immediate and long-term strategies. While boycotts and divestment can provide swift action against harmful practices, sustained political and economic pressure is needed to shift the broader economic systems that allow these practices to persist. Activists must recognize that callout culture is not just about exposing bad behavior, it is about holding individuals and corporations accountable in ways that change the dynamics of power. By organizing around consumer behavior, worker solidarity, and regulatory reforms, we can shift the economic landscape toward one that values human rights, justice, and sustainability above corporate profit.

Helpful Tools

- Buycott

Buycott is an app that allows users to scan barcodes of products to check whether the company behind them supports political causes or practices they might want to boycott. The app has a database of campaigns and causes, letting users track companies based on their environmental, political, or social policies.

- GoodGuide

GoodGuide provides detailed information on products, including health, environmental, and social impact ratings. While it doesn't specifically focus on boycotting, it helps users make more ethical choices by providing insight into how companies perform on various issues like human rights, environmental protection, and labor practices.

- Corporate Accountability

This platform tracks the corporate actions of major companies, especially their environmental and social practices. It focuses on advocating for responsible corporate practices and offers detailed reports on companies that consumers can consider supporting or avoiding based on their values.

- Socially Responsible Investing (SRI) Apps

Several investment apps like Swell Investing, Motif Investing, and Impact Shares help people divest from companies that don't align with ethical or social goals. These apps let users invest in funds or companies that support social justice, environmental sustainability, and other progressive causes.

- Ethical Consumer

This is a website that provides detailed ethical reviews of companies in various industries, from food to electronics. Ethical Consumer highlights which companies are harming the environment, exploiting workers, or involved in controversial political activities, making it easier to choose ethical alternatives.

- Fair Trade Finder

Fair Trade Finder is an app that helps consumers find products and companies that are certified as Fair Trade. Fair Trade certification ensures that companies are adhering to ethical labor practices, environmentally sustainable methods, and are committed to community empowerment.

- Green America's "Green Business Network"

Green America's app helps consumers make more sustainable choices by connecting them with businesses committed to environmental sustainability and social justice. Their app also has tools for identifying companies that harm the planet or communities.

- What's In My Food?

This app helps consumers scan products to see if they contain harmful chemicals or unethical ingredients. While focused on food, it also includes insight into where products come from and which companies support questionable business practices.

- The Good On You App

Good On You is an app focused on ethical fashion. It rates clothing brands based on their impact on the environment, people, and animals. The app provides clear and accessible information about which brands are ethical and sustainable, allowing users to avoid companies that engage in harmful practices, such as poor labor conditions or environmental damage.

- Consumer Reports

While not exclusively a tool for boycotting companies, Consumer Reports provides in-depth research and reviews on products and companies, including their business practices. The platform evaluates product safety, sustainability, and corporate ethics, giving consumers valuable information to guide their purchasing decisions and avoid supporting companies with unethical practices.

Ethical Consumption

Ethical consumption may be inconvenient, but it is one of the most powerful tools available to us in holding corporations accountable. In a world where corporate interests dominate, the only language that truly resonates with these entities is financial loss. For all their claims of social responsibility and sustainability, most companies are driven by profit, not morality. When we make the difficult but essential choice to spend our money on products and services from companies that align with our values, we send a clear message: we will not support businesses that perpetuate harm, inequality, or exploitation.

Inconvenience is part of the price we pay for creating a more just world. Seeking out ethical alternatives often means spending more time researching companies, avoiding convenient, mass-produced goods, and sometimes paying a higher price for sustainable or fair-trade options. It means foregoing products that are cheaper because they exploit workers or degrade the environment. This might feel burdensome, but when we understand that every dollar we spend is a vote for the kind of society we want, the inconvenience becomes a small price to pay for creating lasting change.

It is a moral choice because it directly challenges systems of inequality and exploitation that are often invisible to consumers. Corporations thrive on these systems, cutting corners, underpaying workers, and damaging ecosystems, all while maximizing profits. If they cannot profit off human rights abuses, environmental destruction, or unethical labor practices, they will be forced to reconsider their business models. When we choose to support companies with fair wages, sustainable practices, and ethical labor standards, we are making a statement: the dignity of workers, the health of the planet, and social justice are non-negotiable.

Ultimately, ethical consumption is not just a personal choice but a collective one. If enough of us make the effort to hold companies accountable with our purchasing power, we can create a ripple effect that forces corporations to adopt better practices or face financial ruin. In this capitalist society, it's the only language they understand, and it's the most effective way to demand the change we wish to see.

110

Chapter 10~BUILD
Burn the System Down, Build A New One

As we stand on the precipice of a world in turmoil, a world where the systems that have oppressed and marginalized so many for so long are beginning to unravel, we must face a crucial reality: dismantling the old is not enough. For the revolution to be sustainable, for the world we dream of to take root and grow, we must also build anew. The structures of power that dominate our economies, our governments, and our communities have been built over centuries, and as they crumble, we cannot simply leave the void behind. We must replace them with something better, something that serves the people and not the powerful.

The work of revolution is not just the tearing down of corrupt institutions and harmful systems. It is the painstaking, often quiet work of constructing new ones, ones that embody the values of justice, equity, sustainability, and solidarity. In other words, while we fight to burn down the old, we must also build the new, institutions, infrastructures, and communities that will outlast us and carry forward the vision we are fighting for.

This task is daunting. After all, the systems we are fighting against have had centuries to entrench themselves, to solidify their hold on power, and to create institutions that serve their interests. The idea of creating a new system from the ground up can feel overwhelming, especially when the forces of reaction are constantly pushing back against progress. Yet, the very fact that we are witnessing the collapse of these systems presents an unparalleled opportunity to build something better. We are living in a time where the old ways are being revealed for their flaws, and the need for change is so palpable that it cannot be ignored. This is our chance to create institutions and systems that reflect the needs and desires of all people, not just the wealthy few.

At the heart of building a new world lies the idea of mutual aid. While the dominant systems of capitalism and state control focus on competition, greed, and individualism, mutual aid operates on the principles of cooperation, community, and solidarity. In mutual aid networks, people come together to support one another, offering resources, time, and labor to those in need. It is a framework that sees people not as isolated individuals but as interconnected members of a community, where everyone's well-being is tied to the well-being of the whole. Mutual aid is not a temporary solution to systemic problems; it is the foundation of a new way of living and organizing our societies.

In the face of increasing inequality, environmental destruction, and the erosion of civil rights, mutual aid provides an alternative vision of how we can organize ourselves, one that is rooted in the values of justice, cooperation, and shared responsibility. The traditional systems we have relied on for so long, governments, corporations, institutions, are often the very sources of the problems we face. They are complicit in perpetuating inequality, exploitation, and environmental degradation. Instead of waiting for these systems to reform or collapse on their own, we must actively create new systems that embody the principles of care, solidarity, and sustainability.

One of the greatest strengths of mutual aid is that it is inherently flexible. Unlike top-down, bureaucratic systems that are slow to change and often resistant to new ideas, mutual aid networks can be adapted to fit the needs of the community at any given moment. They can scale from small, grassroots efforts to larger, more complex systems of mutual support. Whether it's organizing a food pantry for a neighborhood or creating a cooperative for workers to own and control their labor, mutual aid allows us to build the infrastructure we need to survive and thrive while the old systems collapse around us.

In building a new world, we must begin with the basics, providing for the immediate needs of our communities. This means establishing systems of food security, healthcare, housing, and education that are not controlled by profit motives but are instead rooted in the principle that every person deserves dignity and access to resources. We must create food cooperatives that prioritize local, sustainable farming and eliminate the exploitation of workers in the food industry. We must ensure that healthcare is treated as a human right, not a commodity to be bought and sold, and that everyone has access to the care they need regardless of their income. Education must be reimagined as a tool for liberation, not just a way to prepare people for the workforce, and housing should be a universal right, not something to be speculated on or hoarded.

At the same time, we must recognize that mutual aid is not just about meeting immediate needs. It is also about challenging the underlying power structures that have created and maintained inequality. By building new institutions, we are not merely replacing old systems, we are actively shifting the balance of power. We are creating institutions that do not operate on the logic of profit but on the logic of shared resources and collective well-being. These institutions will not just serve the needs of individuals, they will build communities that are resilient, cooperative, and committed to justice. They will create the foundation for a world in which everyone can thrive, not just survive.

For mutual aid to work on a large scale, however, it needs to be integrated into every part of our society. This means building networks that link local communities to regional and national movements, creating a unified, collective force that can challenge the power of corporations and state actors. This requires not only grassroots organizing but also political advocacy and activism. Mutual aid, in its most effective form, is not just a survival strategy, it is a revolutionary tool that can reshape society.

A crucial part of this transformation is changing the way we think about power. In the old systems, power is seen as something that is hoarded and wielded by a select few. It is about control, domination, and the accumulation of wealth. But in the new world we are building, power is decentralized. It is distributed among communities, organized through networks of mutual aid, and shared by all. Power is no longer about hoarding resources but about ensuring that everyone has what they need to live a dignified, meaningful life.

This reimagining of power extends beyond just political or economic systems, it includes cultural and social power as well. For far too long, mainstream media, popular culture, and social narratives have been shaped by the interests of the powerful. These narratives tell us what to value, what to believe, and how to behave. To build the new world we want, we must create new cultural institutions, spaces that elevate voices and stories that have been marginalized, that promote creativity, compassion, and justice, and that challenge the dominant cultural norms. This means supporting independent artists, storytellers, and creators who reflect the values of the world we are trying to build. It means fostering a culture of solidarity, of listening and learning from one another, and of creating space for diverse voices to be heard.

In addition, we must consider the environmental dimension of this rebuilding. Our current system of consumption and production is unsustainable and destructive, ravaging ecosystems and exploiting natural resources. As we dismantle the old, we must ensure that the new world we build is rooted in ecological sustainability. This means shifting away from fossil fuels, ending deforestation, and creating systems of agriculture and industry that work in harmony with nature. It is about creating a world where economic growth no longer comes at the expense of the planet but is instead based on principles of regeneration and sustainability.

Building this new world won't be easy, and it won't happen overnight. The systems of oppression, inequality, and exploitation that have existed for so long are deeply entrenched, and they won't disappear without a fight. But that doesn't mean we should shy away from the challenge. We are at a critical juncture in history. The old world is collapsing, and in its place, we have an unprecedented opportunity to create something better, something that can last.

By focusing on mutual aid and building new, just, and sustainable institutions, we are not just creating a world that is more equitable and compassionate, we are creating a world that is resilient, adaptable, and ready to face the challenges of the future. As we fight to dismantle the old systems, we must never forget the importance of building the new. In the end, it is the institutions we create and the communities we build that will outlast us all and carry forward the revolution we are starting today.

Beyond Theory

The task of building a new world doesn't stop at theory. In the previous section, we explored the necessity of creating institutions, infrastructure, and communities that replace the ones being dismantled. But to truly build a world that reflects the values of justice, sustainability, and solidarity, we need to move from theory to practice. This section explores the practical steps required to build the systems that will outlast the old and provide a sustainable foundation for a just society.

Building a new world means constructing institutions that are fundamentally different from the ones that perpetuate inequality and exploitation. In a world dominated by corporate greed, governmental corruption, and social stratification, we must create alternatives that embody cooperation, mutual support, and environmental stewardship. These new institutions will not be built overnight, and they will not emerge without conflict. But they are essential for the future we envision.

To begin, we must understand that creating these new institutions requires both grassroots involvement and strategic organization. While mutual aid and community-based support systems are crucial to the immediate survival of marginalized groups, we must build lasting institutions that function at a larger scale, ones that can replace the current structures of power and address the systemic inequalities built into our economy, government, and social systems.

At the heart of this transformation is the creation of alternative economies, economies that reject the profit-driven motives of traditional capitalism and instead focus on human welfare, environmental sustainability, and equity. These alternative economies are not just theoretical ideals; they are already being built by communities around the world. They include cooperative businesses, community land trusts, local currencies, and other forms of economic cooperation that serve the needs of people instead of corporate interests.

One of the most powerful examples of alternative economies can be seen in the rise of worker cooperatives. Unlike traditional businesses, which are owned by shareholders and run for profit, worker cooperatives are owned and managed by the workers themselves. In these businesses, profits are shared equitably, and decision-making is democratic, meaning that everyone has a voice in how the business is run. This model challenges the hierarchical structure of corporate ownership and ensures that workers are not exploited for the benefit of distant investors.

The cooperative model is not just a workplace arrangement, it is a reflection of a larger vision for how society could operate if we prioritize people over profit. Worker cooperatives provide a tangible alternative to the neoliberal capitalist systems that dominate the global economy. By building more of these businesses, we can create a decentralized economy that operates on the values of solidarity and mutual benefit. This model can be applied to many sectors, from agriculture and manufacturing to healthcare and education, and it can be scaled up to provide broader access to community-driven economic models.

Beyond worker cooperatives, there are other forms of economic activism that are transforming the way we think about wealth, production, and labor. One of these is the concept of community land trusts (CLTs), which focus on providing affordable housing and land access to communities that have been historically excluded from property ownership. CLTs are designed to remove land from the speculative market and put it into community control. This prevents gentrification and ensures that land is used for the benefit of the community rather than for private profit. CLTs can also be part of a broader effort to create localized economies that are self-sustaining and based on shared resources, rather than driven by corporate interests.

Building new institutions also means challenging the financial structures that uphold the current system. We must move away from large, centralized banks that serve the interests of the wealthy and instead build community-based financial institutions such as credit unions, community development financial institutions (CDFIs), and public banks. These institutions can provide loans and financial services to communities that have been shut out by traditional banks, especially low-income individuals and marginalized groups. By supporting these alternative financial institutions, we can begin to dismantle the financial power structures that perpetuate inequality.

116

However, building alternative economies is only one piece of the puzzle. We must also create political systems that reflect our values of justice, equality, and sustainability. This means advocating for policies that redistribute wealth, protect the environment, and ensure access to basic rights for all people. In many ways, this requires us to reclaim the political process from the corporate elite and the wealthy few who have captured it for their own benefit.

One of the most important aspects of this political transformation is the reimagining of democracy itself. In the current system, democracy is often reduced to voting every few years and participating in token public debates. But real democracy is about more than just casting ballots; it's about creating a system of governance where all people have a voice in the decisions that affect their lives. This means fostering participatory decision-making processes at every level, whether it's within our local communities, workplaces, or government institutions.

Participatory democracy can take many forms. It can involve town hall meetings, citizen assemblies, and community forums where people come together to discuss and decide on important issues. It can also include participatory budgeting, where communities have a say in how public funds are spent. In countries like Uruguay and Switzerland, participatory budgeting has already shown the power of this model, allowing citizens to prioritize public spending on projects that serve their needs.

The transformation of political systems must also include the abolition of systems of oppression, whether they are racial, gender-based, or class-based. We must work to dismantle the structures of white supremacy, patriarchy, and capitalism that have shaped our societies for centuries. This requires confronting not only the individual prejudices that exist but also the systemic inequalities that have been built into our institutions, policies, and cultural norms. Real political change must involve the deconstruction of these oppressive systems and the creation of new systems based on equity and justice.

Building new institutions and systems of governance also means rethinking the way we approach global issues, such as climate change, migration, and social justice. The interconnectedness of these issues requires global solidarity, where communities come together to address common problems. The environmental movement, for example, must not only focus on reducing carbon emissions but also on ensuring that the benefits of environmental policies are shared equitably, particularly with communities that are most affected by environmental degradation.

One of the most pressing global issues is climate change, which requires a radical shift in how we produce and consume resources. Building new institutions means embracing renewable energy, reducing waste, and rethinking our relationship with the natural world. The transition to a green economy is not just an environmental necessity; it is an opportunity to build a more just and sustainable world. This means prioritizing the needs of communities that have been disproportionately affected by climate change, such as Indigenous communities, people of color, and low-income populations. It also means creating green jobs, investing in renewable energy infrastructure, and ensuring that climate policies are not just about saving the planet but about creating a fair and equitable future for all.

Another crucial aspect of building new institutions is the need for global solidarity. The challenges we face, whether they are related to climate change, economic inequality, or social justice, are global in scope. The current political and economic systems are organized in a way that allows wealthy nations and corporations to exploit and control the resources of poorer countries. This global system must be dismantled, and new forms of international cooperation must be built on principles of equity, mutual aid, and shared resources.

For example, the movement for global debt relief has gained momentum in recent years, with activists and organizations calling for the cancellation of debts owed by developing countries to wealthy nations and international financial institutions. This debt relief is seen as a necessary step in addressing the global inequality that has been exacerbated by colonialism and imperialism. At the same time, international efforts to ensure fair trade, equitable distribution of resources, and access to healthcare and education must be prioritized. The creation of new international institutions that operate on principles of justice and equity is essential to building a world that works for all people, not just the wealthy few.

As we build these new institutions, we must remember that this work
is ongoing. The systems we are fighting against are deeply entrenched
and will not be dismantled overnight. But by creating alternatives that
are rooted in solidarity, justice, and sustainability, we are laying the
foundation for a better world. The institutions we build today will
serve as the foundation for future generations, and it is our
responsibility to ensure that these institutions are equitable,
democratic, and sustainable.

Ultimately, the work of building new institutions and systems is about
creating a world that is centered on the needs of people and the
planet. It is about rejecting the oppressive structures of power that
have governed our societies for so long and creating systems that
prioritize justice, equality, and sustainability. It is about building the
world we want to live in, not just the world we have been given. This
is the work that will outlast us all, and it is the legacy we must leave
behind.

Cooperative Examples

Several countries and large communities around the world have
embraced cooperative work and culture in various forms, from
worker cooperatives to community-driven economies and governance
systems. These examples illustrate the power of cooperative models in
building solidarity, sustainability, and equitable economic systems.

Here are some notable examples:

Mondragón Corporation (Spain)
Located in the Basque region of Spain, Mondragón is one of the
largest and most successful examples of a worker cooperative
federation in the world. Established in 1956, Mondragón consists of
over 100 cooperatives across various industries, including
manufacturing, retail, finance, and education. The cooperative model
means that workers are also owners of the companies they work for,
sharing profits and participating in decision-making processes. This
model has allowed Mondragón to thrive and maintain stability even
during economic downturns, providing jobs and economic resilience
to the Basque region.

The Emilia-Romagna Region (Italy)
In Italy, the region of Emilia-Romagna is home to a significant
number of worker cooperatives, particularly in the sectors of
agriculture, manufacturing, and services. The cooperative movement
in Emilia-Romagna is one of the most robust in Europe, with
thousands of cooperatives operating in the region. These cooperatives
focus on democratic decision-making, equitable profit-sharing, and
the creation of sustainable and ethical businesses. The region's
commitment to cooperatives has helped create a thriving local
economy based on community values rather than corporate interests.

The Zapatista Communities (Mexico)
In Chiapas, Mexico, the Zapatista movement has built a network of
autonomous communities that operate under cooperative principles.
These communities reject the dominant capitalist economic system
and instead focus on self-governance, mutual aid, and collective
decision-making. The Zapatistas have created a system where
resources are shared among the community, and labor is distributed
equitably. They operate collectively in agriculture, education,
healthcare, and other areas, with a focus on indigenous autonomy
and social justice. The Zapatista communities are a powerful example
of how cooperative work can foster self-determination and resilience
in the face of outside pressures.

Cooperative Housing in Scandinavia
Scandinavian countries, particularly Sweden, Norway, and Denmark,
have a long history of cooperative housing systems, where residents
collectively own and manage their housing units. These cooperatives
are typically organized on the basis of shared responsibility, with
residents participating in the decision-making process and
contributing to the upkeep of the property. This model allows for
affordable and sustainable housing options, as well as community-
building and social cohesion among residents. The cooperative
housing model in these countries has contributed to high levels of
social trust and low rates of homelessness.

Freiburg and the Ecovillage Movement (Germany)
Freiburg, Germany, is known for its commitment to sustainable living
and cooperative projects. The city has embraced renewable energy,
green building practices, and cooperative housing. The Freiburg
Ecovillage, a part of this movement, is an intentional community that

focuses on environmental sustainability, cooperative economics, and social equity. Residents of the Ecovillage live in community-owned buildings, grow food collectively, and share resources to minimize their ecological footprint. The success of Freiburg and similar ecovillages in Germany demonstrates the potential for cooperative work to foster sustainable living and eco-friendly practices.

The Worker Cooperative Movement in the United Kingdom
In the UK, worker cooperatives have gained significant traction, particularly in cities like Bristol and London. These cooperatives span a wide range of industries, from retail and hospitality to media and tech. One notable example is the Co-operative Group, the UK's largest cooperative, which operates in retail, insurance, and funeral care. Additionally, there are many smaller, worker-owned cooperatives that focus on ethical business practices, sustainability, and community empowerment. The UK's cooperative sector emphasizes the potential for shared ownership and democratic management in creating a fairer and more sustainable economy.

The Cooperatives of Kerala (India)
Kerala, a state in southern India, is home to a vast network of cooperatives that operate in various sectors, including agriculture, fisheries, banking, and retail. These cooperatives are credited with helping Kerala achieve high levels of literacy, healthcare, and social welfare. Kerala's cooperative movement, particularly in the agricultural and credit sectors, has empowered marginalized communities, provided financial services to rural areas, and supported local economies. The success of Kerala's cooperatives has been attributed to their inclusive approach, which ensures that the benefits of economic growth are shared among all members of society, not just the wealthy elite.

The Cooperative Movement in Quebec (Canada)
Quebec, Canada, is home to a large and vibrant cooperative movement, with cooperatives operating in various sectors, including agriculture, retail, healthcare, and housing. One of the most prominent examples is Desjardins, the largest cooperative financial institution in North America. Desjardins serves millions of members and focuses on providing ethical financial services, such as loans for small businesses and support for local community projects. In addition to financial cooperatives, Quebec has a thriving cooperative sector in

the food and housing industries, demonstrating the potential for cooperative models to address social and economic challenges.

The Cooperative Movement in Argentina (Argentina)
In Argentina, particularly after the 2001 economic crisis, worker cooperatives began to flourish as a response to widespread job losses and factory closures. In cities like Buenos Aires, workers who had been laid off or displaced from privatized industries took control of abandoned factories and turned them into worker-run cooperatives. One famous example is Fábrica de Cervezas (the Brewery), which became a symbol of workers' resistance and the cooperative movement. These cooperatives represent a radical shift in how business is conducted, emphasizing collective ownership and the reintegration of workers into the decision-making processes of the industries they help run.

The Cooperative Movement in New Zealand
New Zealand has a long history of cooperative models, particularly in agriculture and dairy. The Fonterra Cooperative Group, one of the world's largest dairy exporters, operates on a cooperative model where farmers own and control the company. This allows for more equitable profit distribution and ensures that the benefits of the industry are shared with local farmers rather than corporate shareholders. Additionally, New Zealand has a robust cooperative sector in finance, housing, and retail, with several consumer-owned cooperatives offering affordable and sustainable services to local communities.

The Indigenous Cooperatives in the U.S.
In the U.S., several Indigenous communities have embraced cooperative models as a way to reclaim control over their resources and promote economic sovereignty. One example is the Cooperative Development Institute (CDI), which supports Indigenous communities in the Northeast U.S. in developing their own cooperatives. These cooperatives often focus on cultural preservation, sustainable land management, and providing affordable services to community members. This approach allows Indigenous peoples to combine traditional values of community, sustainability, and cooperation with modern economic tools to build wealth and stability within their communities.

The Transition Towns Movement (Global)
The Transition Towns movement is a grassroots initiative that encourages communities to develop sustainable and self-sufficient local economies in the face of environmental and economic crises. Communities around the world, particularly in the UK, the US, and parts of Europe, have embraced the Transition model, which focuses on local food production, renewable energy, and community-driven projects. The movement advocates for a local, cooperative approach to economic activity, where people work together to reduce their reliance on global supply chains and corporate-controlled systems. Transition Towns aim to create local resilience and sustainability through cooperation and shared responsibility.

These examples highlight that cooperative work and culture are not just ideals, they are practical solutions to the systemic challenges we face. Whether it's worker cooperatives in Spain, mutual aid in Mexico, or cooperative housing in Scandinavia, these communities have shown that cooperation, solidarity, and collective ownership can replace the exploitative models of capitalism. By supporting and expanding cooperative networks, we can build an economy that serves the people, not the powerful. The successes of these movements provide a blueprint for how we can create more just, sustainable, and resilient societies, both locally and globally. As we move forward, the lessons learned from these examples will be crucial in building a future that reflects the values of equity, justice, and mutual support.

Chapter 11~BUILD
Solidarity is the Only Path Forward

In the face of the numerous crises, environmental, economic, political, and social, diverse movements for justice, equality, and human rights have risen in different parts of the world, each responding to specific local struggles. Yet, despite their different contexts, these movements share an essential truth: solidarity is the only path forward. To dismantle the oppressive systems that exploit and marginalize people, we must unite. The 4B Movement—Burn, Ban, Boycott, Build— provides a framework not just for resistance, but for unity in action. By bringing together diverse movements under one banner, we can create a force that cannot be ignored, one that will build the new world we all envision, together.

The idea of unity is not one that should be taken lightly. It is not about erasing differences or silencing dissent. It is about finding common ground and recognizing that our struggles are interconnected. The fight for racial justice is connected to the fight for gender equality, which is connected to the fight for climate justice, which is connected to the fight for workers' rights. These struggles do not exist in isolation, and neither should our movements. To succeed in the long run, we must embrace solidarity, not as a mere slogan but as a fundamental principle that guides every action we take.

The global movements that have shaped the 21st century are diverse and wide-ranging, yet they show us the potential power of solidarity in action. From Chile's constitutional reform movement to the women's rights protests in Iran, these struggles have demonstrated the deep well of collective power that exists when people come together with a shared vision of justice. These movements have not only fought for their immediate demands but have also presented radical alternatives to the status quo. They have shown that it is possible to fight against deeply entrenched systems of oppression and come out victorious, not by focusing solely on isolated issues, but by weaving together a broader tapestry of resistance that recognizes the intersecting nature of oppression.

Chile's constitutional reform movement, for example, is a profound lesson in the power of collective action. In the aftermath of decades of neoliberal economic policies, which had decimated public services, exacerbated inequality, and entrenched corporate power, the people of Chile rose up. The 2019 mass protests against the government's economic policies eventually led to the drafting of a new constitution, one that sought to address not just political grievances but also deep social inequalities. The movement was not a single-issue protest, it encompassed a wide range of demands, from workers' rights to gender equality to environmental justice. It was a movement rooted in solidarity, where people from all walks of life, workers, students, women, indigenous groups, and more, came together to demand a better future. The success of the Chilean protests lies not in the immediate outcome of the reform, but in the fact that people from diverse backgrounds were able to find common ground in their shared struggle against injustice. They understood that their fates were linked, and that true liberation would not come from addressing isolated issues but from transforming the entire system.

Similarly, the women's rights protests in Iran have shown us the transformative power of solidarity across national and ideological lines. Over the past few decades, Iranian women have been at the forefront of the fight for freedom and equality in a society governed by patriarchal laws and authoritarian rule. The struggles of Iranian women are not only about achieving gender equality but are part of a broader movement for democratic rights and freedom of expression. Whether it's fighting against forced hijab laws or calling for greater political freedom, Iranian women have shown that their fight is part of a larger global struggle for human rights. The courage of Iranian women in resisting oppression, despite the threat of violence and imprisonment, is a testament to the power of solidarity in action. Their movement, though deeply rooted in local conditions, is also part of a global struggle for gender equality and human rights. The support and solidarity that they have received from women's movements around the world has helped amplify their voices and build a global network of resistance.

These movements, from Chile to Iran, and many others, demonstrate the immense potential of solidarity in building movements that can challenge the status quo. But solidarity requires more than just an abstract commitment to working together. It requires tangible action, deep listening, and a willingness to share resources, knowledge, and power. It requires breaking down the walls that divide us, whether those walls are based on race, gender, nationality, or class. Solidarity is not just about showing up for others; it's about recognizing that the struggle for justice is indivisible, and that we cannot achieve our collective liberation if we leave anyone behind.

The 4B Movement—Burn, Ban, Boycott, Build—offers a framework for unity across these diverse struggles. The first step, "Burn," is about rejecting the systems that perpetuate oppression. This isn't about literal fire; it's about burning down the false narratives, the institutions, and the systems that allow injustice to thrive. Whether we're burning down the patriarchy, the capitalist system, or the racist structures that permeate society, we must be clear about what we are fighting against. The second step, "Ban," calls for direct action, boycotting harmful companies, challenging political systems, and refusing to support organizations that contribute to the problem. This is about putting our economic power to work. The third step, "Boycott," reinforces this idea, pushing us to divest from companies, banks, and institutions that profit off of harm, whether through environmental destruction, exploitation of workers, or support for oppressive governments. Finally, "Build" is the call to create new systems, institutions, and communities that can serve as alternatives to the broken ones we're dismantling. We must build networks of support, cooperative economies, and systems of governance that center care, justice, and sustainability.

To unite diverse movements under the 4B banner, we must recognize that these steps, burning, banning, boycotting, and building, are not isolated from one another. They are interconnected, and they must be approached with an understanding that our struggles are all part of a larger fight for liberation. The fight against environmental degradation is inextricably linked to the fight against racial injustice, which is linked to the fight for women's rights, and so on. To be effective, we must draw these connections and work together to dismantle the systems that benefit the few at the expense of the many.

In order to unify these movements, we need to build coalitions that are grounded in respect, mutual support, and a shared understanding of the larger goal. This requires engaging with one another, learning from each other's struggles, and understanding that our liberation is tied to the liberation of all. It means recognizing that the fight for justice is not a zero-sum game, and that when one of us wins, we all win. This is the essence of solidarity.

Global struggles, like those seen in Chile and Iran, offer valuable lessons for us as we build our own movement for justice. These struggles show us that victory is possible when we come together, when we share our resources and wisdom, and when we stay committed to the long-term process of building a better world. The road ahead will be difficult, and the forces we face are powerful, but as long as we stay united, as long as we act in solidarity with one another, we will be unstoppable.

To build a movement that outlasts us all, we must focus on unity, not just for the sake of unity, but because it is essential for the success of the broader struggle. The 4B Movement provides the framework to unite diverse movements, to challenge the systems of oppression, and to build a new world from the ashes of the old. This is not just about today; it's about creating a legacy that will carry us through the generations to come. Solidarity is the only path forward because without it, we are divided, and divided we cannot win. Together, we can burn down the old systems, banish their power, boycott their greed, and build something new, a world that is just, equitable, and sustainable for all.

To deepen the conversation on solidarity and its role in unifying diverse movements, it is crucial to recognize that solidarity isn't merely about physical presence or speaking in unison, it's about fostering a deep, strategic, and consistent commitment to the collective struggle. True solidarity requires a willingness to show up not just when it's convenient, but especially when it's difficult, uncomfortable, or challenging. It means standing with others when their struggles intersect with your own, even if their specific battles seem distant or unrelated to your immediate concerns. It means showing up in moments of crisis, but also in moments of mundane, everyday struggle, as these are often the moments that define the long-term success of movements.

Solidarity is about understanding that your fight is never just for yourself, but for the collective. It involves recognizing that the fight for women's rights cannot succeed if it is disconnected from the fight for racial justice, environmental justice, labor rights, or indigenous rights. It's about weaving together the threads of these struggles into one strong, unified fabric. By actively listening to the voices of marginalized groups, supporting their demands, and amplifying their struggles, we can create a movement that is not only diverse but also deeply rooted in empathy and mutual respect. The more inclusive our movement, the stronger it will be, as it will draw upon the diverse perspectives, strategies, and strengths of all involved.

To truly unify diverse movements under the 4B banner, we must practice the values we preach, equality, justice, and respect, every day. This means committing to inclusivity in the way we organize, the language we use, and the spaces we create. It means being mindful of the ways in which we, sometimes unintentionally, replicate systems of oppression, even within our own movements. To dismantle the systems of oppression outside, we must first challenge those same systems within, ensuring that our struggle for liberation is holistic and rooted in true, unyielding solidarity.

This requires not only coming together on specific issues but also supporting long-term, systemic change. It's about not just fighting the immediate battle but building a broader, unified movement that can create and support lasting change. Movements like those in Chile and Iran are clear examples of this. They show us that while immediate demands are essential, true transformation comes from sustained, collective effort across multiple fronts, from grassroots organizing to political advocacy, from cultural change to the creation of alternative institutions. Solidarity is the connective tissue that holds these varied efforts together, making them stronger and more resilient against the forces of oppression.

Through solidarity, we recognize that our liberation is tied to the liberation of all people. And as we unite under the 4B banner, we must also remember that this work is never just about winning small battles, it is about changing the conditions that allow injustice to thrive. It is about rewriting the very rules that govern our societies, economies, and lives. Only through collective, unified action can we hope to dismantle these systems and build something better, something just, and something sustainable. Solidarity is not just the path forward, it is the only path forward.

Chapter 12~BUILD
Where Are the Men? Who Cares.

Throughout history, the involvement of men in feminist movements has been a double-edged sword. On the one hand, many men have fought valiantly for the liberation of women, standing alongside their sisters in the struggle against patriarchy, inequality, and oppression. On the other hand, there is a long and well-documented history of men co-opting feminist agendas for their own purposes, watering down the radical demands of women's liberation, or using the feminist movement as a vehicle for their own power and gain. The question is not whether men should be involved in feminist movements, but how. More specifically, the question is how men can support the movement without overshadowing or undermining the voices of those who have been, and continue to be, oppressed by systems of patriarchy. The answer lies in a delicate balance: men must support, but never lead.

It is essential to understand that the feminist movement is, at its core, a movement for the liberation of women, and for the dismantling of systems that oppress women and gender minorities. The goal of feminism is not to achieve some abstract notion of equality with men, but to radically reimagine a world where the structures of power, economic, political, and social, are no longer based on patriarchy. Men, as the primary beneficiaries of these structures, must recognize their role in perpetuating them and resist the urge to lead the charge in the fight for women's liberation. In fact, history has shown that when men have taken leadership roles in feminist movements, the radical potential of these movements has often been diluted or diverted into more palatable, less threatening forms that uphold the status quo.

Men have often entered feminist spaces with good intentions, but their presence has not always served the cause. One of the dangers of male involvement in feminist movements is the tendency to steer the conversation back to what men perceive as the "right" way to achieve change. This often leads to a re-framing of feminist goals that prioritizes male comfort and perspectives, rather than centering the lived experiences of women. Men have a history of determining what feminist success should look like, whether it's more female representation in political office or equal pay in corporate spaces, without fully understanding the radical rethinking of power dynamics that feminism demands. These are important goals, of course, but they are not the end-all-be-all of feminist liberation. If men are allowed to co-opt the feminist agenda, we risk watering down its true essence: the dismantling of patriarchy in all its forms.

This co-optation is not limited to the political realm. It has seeped into the cultural and social dimensions of feminism as well. For years, men have been allowed to define what women's liberation should look like in media, literature, and popular culture. Men often tell the stories of women's struggles, not from the perspective of liberation, but from the perspective of what men are willing to tolerate or accept. Even today, the mainstream feminist narrative is often one shaped by male voices, sometimes without even realizing it. This is where the subtle dangers of male involvement in feminism lie: in the erasure or distortion of women's own voices. Men must understand that while their support is valuable, they must resist the urge to define the terms of the struggle. It is not their place to set the agenda or to decide which issues are most important for feminist movements. Instead, men must listen, learn, and support the leadership of women and gender minorities who have been most directly affected by patriarchy.

The history of male allies in feminist movements is filled with examples of good intentions gone wrong. In the early 20th century, for instance, many male leaders were involved in the suffrage movement, advocating for women's right to vote. However, the suffrage movement itself often excluded women of color, working-class women, and other marginalized groups, and was often led by upper-class white women. Male allies were instrumental in pushing for the vote, but in doing so, they frequently prioritized the needs of white women over those of women of color and other marginalized groups. This is not to say that men should not be allies in the feminist movement, but it serves as a cautionary tale about the dangers of men taking the lead in spaces that are supposed to be about women's liberation. It is important to recognize that the feminism of wealthy, white women has historically been different from the feminism of working-class women, Black women, Indigenous women, and women of color. Men, even when they have the best intentions, must be careful not to erase these critical distinctions or to overshadow the voices of women from historically oppressed groups.

In more recent history, we have seen similar dynamics play out in the wake of movements like #MeToo. Men have been vocal in their support for the movement, but at times their involvement has obscured the voices of women who were the original sources of the movement's power. The #MeToo movement, while incredibly important in giving women a platform to speak out against sexual harassment and abuse, has also been marked by the heavy presence of male figures in leadership roles, who have occasionally diverted the conversation toward issues of male accountability or reformed masculinity. While it is vital that men examine their own roles in perpetuating systems of gender-based violence, the leadership of women must remain front and center. Men should be the supporters, not the leaders, of these movements.

When men take leadership roles in feminist movements, they often bring with them their own unconscious biases, internalized patriarchal attitudes, and assumptions about what is possible. For example, a man may enter a feminist space with the belief that the movement's goal should be a world where men and women are "equal," without acknowledging the deep-rooted inequalities that exist in society. This can lead to a desire for compromise, for finding middle ground that benefits everyone, but this approach can water down the movement's radical demands. The goal of feminism is not to create equal opportunities within a fundamentally unjust system but to radically transform that system so that it no longer perpetuates inequality in the first place. Men, in their support, should prioritize listening to women's voices, acknowledging the diversity of feminist thought, and understanding that true equality cannot be achieved by simply tweaking the system, it must be overthrown.

There is also the issue of the power dynamic. Men, even in their support of feminism, still often hold power in ways that women do not. This power dynamic is deeply embedded in the way society is structured. Even progressive men in feminist spaces can unintentionally reinforce this hierarchy by dominating conversations, making decisions for the group, or assuming leadership roles. Feminism, to be truly liberating, must be a movement that challenges these power structures, not one that inadvertently upholds them. Male allies must be aware of the privileges they hold and must actively work to redistribute that power, stepping aside when necessary to ensure that women's voices are heard and their leadership is acknowledged.

This is not to say that men have no role in feminist movements, nor is it an attempt to exclude them. Men must support feminist movements, but their support must always be in a way that amplifies, rather than silences, women's voices. They must understand that feminism is not about inclusion in a movement that has historically centered male perspectives, it is about transforming society in ways that benefit women, and particularly women of color, working-class women, and those from other marginalized communities. Men must never lead feminist movements; they must always follow the leadership of women, and in doing so, they must commit to dismantling the systems of power and privilege that have long kept women from fully realizing their potential.

Ultimately, the question of where the men are, and why it matters, boils down to this: men must be present, but only in service of the movement. Their role is to support, not to direct, and their voices must always be secondary to the voices of women and gender minorities who have been historically oppressed by patriarchy. Men must understand that their liberation is tied to the liberation of women, but they must be careful not to assume the leadership that rightfully belongs to those who have borne the weight of patriarchal oppression. It is through this humility, this willingness to listen and follow, that men can truly contribute to the feminist cause. For the feminist movement to remain true to its radical roots, it must always be led by the voices of those who have suffered under the systems it seeks to dismantle.

Men who genuinely care about feminism must understand that the movement is not about them. It is about women, it is about justice, and it is about building a world where all people, regardless of gender, are free from the chains of oppression. They must support with the understanding that feminism is about dismantling the systems of power that have historically privileged men and, in doing so, create a world where the full humanity of women is recognized and honored. Solidarity with the feminist movement is essential, but leadership within it must belong to those who have been most directly harmed by the systems of patriarchy. Only then can we begin to build a truly just and equal world.

Men who genuinely wish to support feminism must also recognize that their role is not to define the movement's goals or narrative. Their primary responsibility is to work toward dismantling the systems that have long protected their privileges, while elevating the voices of those most impacted by oppression. Men must act as allies by stepping back from positions of leadership and allowing women, particularly women of color, to take the reins. This shift is not only about practical action but also about confronting internalized patriarchal ideas that can subtly influence how men engage with feminism. The goal is not just the removal of overt sexist behavior but the cultivation of a culture in which women are seen as equal leaders in the fight for their own liberation.

The feminist movement, at its core, is a movement of women asserting their right to autonomy, dignity, and control over their bodies, lives, and futures. It's critical for men to understand that these goals cannot be truly achieved unless they support the dismantling of patriarchal structures and empower women to define their own terms of liberation. Men must work alongside feminists, not in competition or with the desire to be seen as "better" allies but with a recognition of their role in society and a commitment to creating space for women's leadership. This support is not only beneficial for feminism but for society at large, as it challenges traditional gender roles and opens the door to a more equitable world for all genders.

For real change to occur, men must reflect on how deeply patriarchy has shaped their lives and challenge their own behaviors. By recognizing the nuances of gender inequality and standing in solidarity with women's leadership, men contribute meaningfully to the feminist cause. But they must always do so with the understanding that their role is to support, not lead, the revolution. True feminism requires that men take on the responsibility of breaking down their privileges and empowering women to take the lead in their own liberation. Without this shift, the movement risks remaining incomplete and diluted. Only through these actions can feminism continue to grow and evolve into the transformative force it has always been.

Chapter 13~BUILD
The Future is Female

For thousands of years, men have held the reins of power, steering the course of civilization. They've constructed systems, built empires, and shaped societies in their image. But the results of their leadership are unmistakable: humanity and the planet are teetering on the brink of ruin. The systems that men have built, propped up by their grasp on power, have led us to a point of no return, a point where even the survival of the Earth itself is uncertain. The evidence is all around us: ecological collapse, a global climate crisis, rampant inequality, and a profound breakdown in social cohesion. The systems of patriarchy, capitalism, and exploitation have long perpetuated the idea that men are the rightful stewards of the world, the ones who know best, the ones who are destined to lead. Yet, after thousands of years of male leadership, the world we inhabit today is a fractured, polluted, and increasingly hostile place. Men have had their shot, and they've failed, not just for women, but for everyone. They have run the world into the ground, and now it is time for a change. The future must be in the hands of those who have been systematically excluded from power, women.

The male-dominated systems that have shaped the world are built on a foundation of exploitation, subjugation, and greed. Religion has long been used as one of the most powerful tools to justify male dominance. For centuries, religious doctrines have been manipulated to support the patriarchal order, claiming divine authority for men's control over women. Women have been told, time and again, that their place in society is subservient to men, that their voices do not matter, and that their rights and liberties are to be restricted in the name of God. This religious justification for women's oppression has been used to enforce laws, dictate societal norms, and enforce rigid gender roles that have kept women in their place. Women have been told that their worth is defined by their relationship to men, whether as wives, daughters, or mothers, and that their lives are meant to serve the needs and desires of men. These religious precepts have not just limited women's freedoms, they have erased their humanity, reduced them to second-class citizens, and perpetuated systems that have kept them from realizing their full potential.

The historical use of religion to subjugate women is not an isolated phenomenon. It is woven into the very fabric of patriarchy itself. In societies across the globe, religion has been invoked to maintain control over women, to keep them in check, and to justify male supremacy. Whether it's the Christian notion of women's subordination to men as "the head of the household," or the Islamic interpretation of women's modesty and submission, or the ancient patriarchal deities of Greece and Rome who decreed women to be inferior to men, the justification has always been the same: women are not equal to men, and their role in society is secondary. This religious sanctioning of female subjugation has made it harder to challenge these systems, to question the structures of power that have kept women oppressed for centuries. The divine right of men to lead has been etched into the very consciousness of society, making it seem like an unquestionable fact, an immutable law of nature.

But the problem is that these patriarchal systems, built on the backs of religious oppression and male dominance, are now causing untold harm, not just to women, but to the planet, to society, and even to the men who have benefited from them. The capitalist system that men have created, a system rooted in competition, greed, and exploitation, has eroded the very fabric of human empathy. Under capitalism, survival is a zero-sum game. It teaches that there is not enough for everyone, that success must come at the expense of others, and that the rich and powerful are entitled to more, while the poor are left to fight for scraps. In this system, empathy is not a virtue but a liability. Men, in their pursuit of power, wealth, and dominance, have created a world where caring for others is seen as weak, where cooperation is replaced by ruthless competition, and where human relationships are transactional. People are reduced to commodities, their value determined by their ability to contribute to the economic machine, to serve the interests of the few who hold the power. Capitalism has turned empathy into an endangered species. It has hollowed out human connections, leaving behind a society where loneliness, alienation, and despair have become the norm.

The crisis facing men today is a direct result of the system they have created. The rise of what has been termed "deaths of despair," the surge in suicides, drug overdoses, and alcohol-related deaths among men, is a tragic consequence of the emptiness that capitalism has created. Men have been taught that success is measured by wealth, power, and status, and when they fail to meet these standards, they are left with nothing. The idea that they must compete with other men, that they must be tough, unfeeling, and self-sufficient, has led to a crisis of male mental health. Men are often isolated in their suffering, unable to express vulnerability, unable to ask for help, because society tells them that to do so is to show weakness. The loneliness epidemic among men is a direct result of the patriarchal values that have shaped their lives. They have been taught to suppress their emotions, to reject empathy, and to isolate themselves from others. This has created a generation of men who are disconnected from their own feelings, from their families, and from their communities. They have been taught that their value lies in their ability to dominate, to control, to succeed at any cost, and when they fail to meet these impossible standards, they fall into despair.

This crisis is not just about men's mental health. It is about the failure of the systems that have been created to serve the interests of men, to uphold their power and privilege, and to perpetuate a world where women are subjugated and the planet is destroyed. These systems have not only failed women, people of color, and marginalized communities, they have failed men too. Men are trapped in a system that values their labor but not their humanity. A system that tells them they must work harder, compete more fiercely, and sacrifice their emotional well-being for the sake of economic survival. A system that exploits their bodies and minds until they break. A system that leaves them isolated, disconnected, and unable to form meaningful relationships or find true fulfillment.

This is why the future must not just be about achieving gender equality. It must be about women taking over, women stepping into leadership roles, not just in the home, but in every aspect of society. Women must rise, not just to find equality with men, but to dismantle the systems of patriarchy, capitalism, and oppression that have caused so much harm. Men have had their shot, and they have failed. The systems they've created have driven the planet to the edge of collapse, have destroyed social bonds, and have perpetuated inequality and injustice. Now it's time for women to lead, to build a world based on compassion, cooperation, and sustainability.

Women have long been the caretakers, the nurturers, the ones who have held families and communities together. They have always carried the weight of society's well-being on their shoulders, often without recognition or reward. Now it's time for women to take that leadership into the broader world, to challenge the systems of power that have held them back, and to build something better. The future cannot be one where men continue to cling to power, perpetuating the same broken systems. It must be one where women rise, take control, and rebuild society from the ground up.

Women are not just seeking equality; they are seeking the power to create a world that works for everyone. A world where human connections are valued, where empathy is celebrated, and where the Earth is protected. Women have the compassion, the vision, and the resilience needed to lead us into the future. The future is female, not because women are better than men, but because it's the only way forward. Men have had their shot, and they have failed. It's time for women to rise and take control, to burn down the systems that no longer serve humanity, and to build a world rooted in justice, equity, and sustainability. Only through this radical shift in power can we hope to create a world that is truly just for all.

As the planet teeters on the edge of catastrophe, the need for women to take control of leadership is more urgent than ever. The systems that have shaped our world have been built upon the ideologies of male supremacy, which have historically marginalized women and perpetuated inequality, all while advancing the interests of a small male elite. Men have been at the helm for centuries, and it has become abundantly clear that their approach to governance, whether political, economic, or social, has been profoundly flawed. The very systems they've put in place, capitalism, patriarchy, the exploitation of natural resources, have not only endangered the planet but have also caused irreparable harm to the social fabric of society. And yet, men, despite their repeated failures, continue to cling to power, resistant to the kind of radical change that could save us all.

There is no denying that men have had their chance to lead, and they've systematically failed. Throughout history, male-dominated systems have been justified by the belief that men are inherently more capable, more rational, and more suited for leadership. This belief has been reinforced through religious and cultural narratives that position women as inferior, weaker, and more prone to irrationality or emotional decision-making. These systems, deeply entrenched over thousands of years, have served to suppress women and deny them the opportunity to participate equally in decision-making processes. And yet, despite their dominance, men have consistently steered the world into chaos. Wars have ravaged nations, economies have collapsed, and entire ecosystems have been destroyed, all under male leadership. Men have driven our societies and our planet to the edge of collapse, and yet they remain in charge, insisting on their right to continue leading.

Religion has long been a powerful tool in maintaining male dominance. Across many cultures and societies, religious teachings have been used to justify the subjugation of women, with doctrines that paint women as morally weaker and in need of male guidance and control. These teachings are not just spiritual or theological in nature, they have been woven into the very fabric of societal norms and legal systems. Religious institutions, which were predominantly male-controlled, perpetuated the idea that women's primary role was to serve men, whether as wives, mothers, or caretakers, and that their voices, aspirations, and autonomy should be subordinate to those of men. Religion was used to create and reinforce the belief that men were the natural leaders, with women relegated to the background, limited in their rights and freedoms, and excluded from the most significant decisions of society.

Even today, religion remains a potent tool for the oppression of women. In many parts of the world, women are still denied their fundamental rights in the name of religious dogma. Women are told what they can wear, who they can marry, when and how they can express their sexuality, and how they can live their lives, all under the guise of religious justification. But the truth is, these religious systems were never about spirituality or moral righteousness; they were about control. Men used religion as a means of maintaining power, perpetuating their dominance, and keeping women in a state of subjugation. It is not just the oppression of women that these systems have fostered, but the decay of empathy, the erosion of shared responsibility, and the collapse of communities.

The capitalist system, which is inseparable from patriarchal structures, has further entrenched these dynamics. Capitalism is built on the foundation of endless competition, extraction, and exploitation. It thrives on the idea that individuals must fight for their survival, that human value is determined by one's ability to produce, consume, and compete. The system is designed to pit people against each other, to create winners and losers, and to prioritize profit above all else, including human lives and the environment. This cutthroat survivalist mentality has had a devastating impact on society, making empathy a scarce resource. Under capitalism, empathy is seen as a weakness. In a world where success is determined by how much wealth one can amass, there is no room for compassion, no space for the collective good. The structures that men have created prioritize their own wealth and comfort while the rest of the world is left to fight for scraps.

Women, on the other hand, have always been the ones to carry the weight of empathy. They are the caregivers, the nurturers, the ones who tend to the emotional and social needs of their families and communities. It is women who have been the backbone of society, often working tirelessly, often without recognition, to hold the fabric of society together. Yet, despite this, women have been excluded from positions of power, from decision-making processes, and from the leadership roles that would allow them to shape the future of the world. It is time for this to change. Women have demonstrated time and again that their leadership is rooted in compassion, empathy, and a commitment to the well-being of all people. They have been the ones to keep the world running while men have destroyed it.

The argument for women to take over leadership is not about seeking revenge or asserting dominance, it is about restoring balance. It is about taking back control from a system that has left the world in shambles, a system that has caused immense suffering not just for women but for men as well. The epidemic of male loneliness, the surge in suicides, drug overdoses, and alcohol-related deaths among men, is a direct result of the hollow society that men have created. Men have been taught that their value lies in their ability to compete, to win, to conquer. This hyper-competitive, emotionally repressed model of masculinity has created a society where men are isolated, emotionally disconnected, and alienated from one another. They have been encouraged to suppress their emotions, to bury their vulnerability, and to reject empathy as a weakness. The consequences of this have been devastating. Men are suffering because the systems they created do not allow them to live fully, to express their emotions, or to build the meaningful connections that are necessary for mental and emotional well-being.

This is a crisis of male creation. Men built the world that teaches them to suppress their feelings, to isolate themselves, and to define their worth by their economic success. And when they inevitably fail to meet the impossible standards set by the very system they designed, they fall into despair. They turn to self-destructive behaviors, substance abuse, suicide, violence, to cope with the emotional void created by a system that tells them their humanity is secondary to their productivity. This is the legacy of male leadership: a society that values profit over people, success over empathy, and competition over connection. Men have run the show, and they have created a world that is toxic to everyone, including themselves.

This is why women must not only fight for equality but for power. Women have been excluded from leadership for centuries, but their time has come. It is not enough for women to seek parity with men in the existing structures. Those structures, capitalism, patriarchy, religious dogma, have failed us all. Women must rise to take control, to rebuild the world from the ground up. Women have demonstrated the kind of leadership the world needs: leadership rooted in empathy, compassion, and a commitment to the collective good. Women must lead not because they are inherently better than men, but because they are the ones who have been excluded from the systems that have brought us to this point. Women must take the reins, not just to ensure that women's voices are heard, but to ensure that humanity itself can survive.

The future is female, not because women are inherently superior, but because the systems men have created have led us to the brink of disaster. Men have had their shot, and they have failed. It is time for women to rise, to lead, and to take control of the future. Women have the empathy, the compassion, and the resilience needed to fix the mess men have made. It is time for a radical shift in power. The future of the planet, of humanity, and of justice is in the hands of women, and it is time for women to take that power. The time for change is now. No comprise.

Chapter 14~BUILD
A Global Struggle

Across the world, women are fighting for their rights, their freedom, dignity. Whether in Poland, India, Afghanistan, or any other country, the struggles they face share striking similarities. In each of these places, women are fighting not only against oppressive patriarchal systems but also against authoritarian regimes that seek to control them, physically, emotionally, and economically. These struggles transcend borders because the forces that oppress women are global in scope. Patriarchy, in its most authoritarian form, is not limited by geography. It is a disease that spreads across nations, cultures, and religions, taking root in societies where power is concentrated in the hands of a few men. Women around the world are battling the same forces, despite the different forms those forces may take in different regions. The fight is one, and it is borderless.

In Poland, the government has used its power to restrict women's rights, particularly regarding reproductive freedom. In 2020, the Polish government, in collaboration with the Catholic Church, enacted a near-total abortion ban, making it nearly impossible for women to access abortion care in any circumstance. The law was designed to suppress women's autonomy over their bodies and reinforce the role of women as subordinates to the religious and patriarchal authority of the state. However, women across Poland took to the streets in one of the largest protests the country had ever seen. Thousands of women, along with their allies, protested against the law, demanding the right to make decisions about their bodies. They used their collective power to stand up to the authoritarian government and reject the patriarchal notion that men, and in this case, the church, could control their reproductive rights. Despite the government's attempts to silence them, the women's movement has gained significant traction, and the protests are far from over. Polish women are proving that they will not be subjugated, that they will fight for their autonomy, and that their voices cannot be erased.

Meanwhile, in India, women have been fighting against both cultural patriarchy and an authoritarian government that seeks to suppress their freedoms. India, with its complex cultural landscape and deep-seated gender inequalities, has seen women on the front lines of numerous struggles, from domestic violence to dowry-related deaths, to the fight for equal pay. The rise of Narendra Modi's government has only intensified these battles, as the government increasingly uses religious nationalism to push a patriarchal agenda. Women's rights activists have been met with repression, with police brutality, arbitrary arrests, and even deaths in some cases. Yet, despite this, women have organized and mobilized like never before. Whether it's through the historic farmers' protests in 2020, where women stood shoulder to shoulder with farmers demanding better rights and protections, or through the fight for sexual violence victims' rights, women in India have been relentless in their pursuit of justice. Their struggle is not just for equal representation in the workplace or access to education, it is for a complete reordering of societal norms, an end to patriarchal violence, and the establishment of a government that will protect, rather than persecute, its women.

In Afghanistan, the struggle for women's rights has been both a battle against authoritarian patriarchy and a fight for survival. For two decades, Afghan women fought for basic rights under a new government that promised freedoms, education, and health care. But when the U.S. withdrew from the country and the Taliban returned to power in 2021, these hard-won rights were quickly dismantled. Women were once again forced to stay in their homes, denied access to education, work, and political participation. Yet, even in the face of such repression, Afghan women have not been silenced. They have been organizing, using secret networks to educate girls, to resist the Taliban's restrictions, and to advocate for their rights. The bravery and resilience of Afghan women in the face of such extreme oppression is a testament to the universal struggle for freedom. They know that this fight is far from over, and even in the most dangerous of circumstances, they continue to demand their right to exist as equal citizens, to live freely, and to be in charge of their own bodies and destinies.

These case studies, though distinct in their cultural and political contexts, all point to a common truth: women everywhere are fighting against the same forces of authoritarian patriarchy, which seeks to limit their autonomy, control their bodies, and strip them of their rights. The struggles in Poland, India, Afghanistan, and beyond are not isolated incidents, they are part of a larger global fight for women's liberation. These struggles transcend national borders because the forces that oppress women are interconnected, and they are part of a global network of power that maintains patriarchy, religious control, and economic exploitation. The struggle for women's rights is a global struggle, and it requires solidarity across borders. Women everywhere are fighting for the same fundamental rights: the right to control their bodies, the right to live free from violence and oppression, and the right to have a say in the decisions that shape their lives.

The fight against authoritarian patriarchy is borderless because patriarchy itself is borderless. It is a global system that takes on different forms but is rooted in the same fundamental belief: that men should hold power over women. The fight for women's rights is not just about individual legal victories, such as access to abortion or the right to work, it is about dismantling the entire system of patriarchy, which is perpetuated by religious, economic, and political forces. The struggle is universal because the same forces that oppress women in one country are the same forces that oppress women in every country. The fight against authoritarian patriarchy is a fight against the systems of power that have entrenched gender inequality for millennia. It is a fight to create a world where women's voices are heard, where their bodies are free from control, and where they are able to live full, equal lives alongside men. And that fight, while shaped by local circumstances, is ultimately a global one.

Chapter 15~BUILD
A 4B Implementation Manual

The 4B Movement—Burn, Ban, Boycott, Build—offers a strategic framework for dismantling oppressive systems and replacing them with structures rooted in justice, equality, and sustainability. The foundation of this movement lies in creating local chapters that bring the 4B strategy to life in communities. These chapters are critical for organizing action, mobilizing people, and challenging systems of oppression, starting with identifying the most urgent issues in the community.

Creating a local 4B chapter begins with assembling a committed leadership team. This team must be diverse in perspective and skill, ensuring inclusivity and effectiveness. Once the leadership team is in place, the next step is to define the mission based on the needs of the community. Whether it's gender inequality, racial injustice, environmental degradation, or economic exploitation, identifying specific, actionable issues will guide the chapter's work and provide focus.

The first phase of the 4B strategy, Burn, involves rejecting the systems of exploitation and oppression. Locally, this means organizing protests, strikes, and disruptions that challenge the status quo. Target corrupt local officials, harmful businesses, and discriminatory systems directly. These actions should be organized and strategic, aiming to send a clear message to those in power that their control is no longer unquestioned. It's not just about raising awareness but about demanding specific, actionable change.

Following the Burn phase, the Ban phase takes action by targeting businesses and organizations that profit from exploitation. Boycotts are a powerful tool here. A successful boycott involves mobilizing a broad coalition of activists, consumers, and workers who can collectively disrupt the profits of harmful institutions. Public awareness campaigns help educate people on why the boycott matters and how their participation contributes to meaningful change.

Simultaneously, effective media campaigns amplify the movement's message. Use social media, local newspapers, and radio stations to share the movement's goals, amplify marginalized voices, and call for action. Media serves as a tool for building solidarity and gaining broader support, helping to sustain momentum and pressure those in power.

Finally, the Build phase is about creating alternatives, cooperative businesses, mutual aid networks, and community organizations that prioritize the collective good. These alternatives offer solutions to the problems identified in the earlier phases and help build sustainable systems that can replace the old ones. The Build phase ensures the movement isn't just about resistance but about proactively creating a better future.

By organizing locally and connecting with other 4B chapters globally, the movement gains strength and amplifies its impact. Each phase of the 4B strategy works together to challenge oppression, disrupt harmful systems, and build new, equitable institutions. Through persistence and collaboration, the 4B Movement can create lasting change.

What about Sex? No More Mrs. Nice. Or Mrs. at all?

Sex is not a duty; it's a kindness. Let me make this clear: it is not your job to evolve men, to shape them into kinder, more humane creatures. It is not your responsibility to turn them into decent human beings, better leaders, or people who even understand the concept of doing no harm and helping others. Oh, what a revolutionary idea that would be. Instead, all we get is violence, the theft of our basic rights, and the constant attempts to keep us down at every turn. Men try to hold you in place and tell you to like it, and worse, they try to convince you there's nothing you can do about it.

You hold the most valuable currency on this planet, and it's a currency they want. They want it so badly, they will traffic you, assault you, murder you, deny you your rights, rape you, beat you, hold you hostage in the name of religion, and cover up the violence with the same excuse. They want to control you, reduce you to a vessel, a commodity, something to be bought, sold, or discarded. It's all about ownership. Since that certain book was written, they've been hunting your innate power, autonomy, and strength. There's a reason we're the givers of life. And there's a reason they've tried to suppress us for so long: because with that power, we can take it all back. And let me tell you, silence is a vote. Silence is complicity. Silence means accepting their control over you.

Not all of them, no. But those who do not fight for us, who do not stand up for you, for all of us, they deserve nothing. Not a damn thing. They don't deserve a smile, not on the street, not in the home, not a second of your time. They don't deserve dinner at the table, respect, or any obedience. Not now, not ever. Not until they change their ways. And let's be clear, most of them won't, unless we force them to. Right now, they hold the power. They have the control. And their plans for us are terrifying. They are winning, for now, but this battle is just the beginning. The war is on our terms, and it's just getting started.

It's taken far too long. Decades, centuries. Generations of suffering. And those who tell you to just play along, to vote harder, to join a group, including this book and previous section, that's exactly what they want you to do. So you must do more. They want you to play by the old rules. But those rules are the baseline, the starting point. They are what got us here, and they're not enough anymore. Those old rules are a trap. We will no longer play by them. They mean us harm, we will not accept it. We will withhold our kindness, our comfort, our love, our compassion, our sex, our marriages, until they deserve it.

More to come…

Chapter 16~BUILD
Forming a Multi-Generational Plan

The struggle for justice and equality is never easy, and it is certainly never quick. While the need for urgent action is undeniable, the long-term process of change can often feel like a slow grind, one that tests the limits of patience, resilience, and determination. In a world where we are conditioned to expect immediate results, where success is often measured by quick wins and fast rewards, it is easy to become disillusioned when change seems too slow or too difficult. But true transformation, especially on the scale we are talking about, dismantling centuries of patriarchy, capitalist exploitation, and systemic oppression, is not something that happens overnight. It is a slow, deliberate process that requires persistence, strategy, and a willingness to push through the inevitable setbacks and challenges that will arise along the way. Persistence matters more than quick wins because the systems we are fighting against are deeply entrenched, and they will not be dismantled by a single protest, a fleeting hashtag, or an isolated victory. To win in the long run, we must understand that the path to true change is a marathon, not a sprint.

We live in an age where instant gratification has become the norm, thanks in part to the digital age and the rapid flow of information. Social media campaigns can spread in a matter of minutes, and viral moments can make us feel like we are part of something bigger than ourselves, that change is just around the corner. But quick fixes rarely lead to lasting change. When we focus too much on the immediate, we risk overlooking the deeper, structural changes that need to be made. The fight for women's liberation, racial justice, environmental sustainability, and economic equity is not just about fighting for rights, it is about fundamentally altering the way society is structured, how power is distributed, and how resources are allocated. These are not changes that can be achieved in a matter of weeks or months. They require years, even decades, of persistent effort, of organizing, of challenging entrenched systems, and of refusing to give up even when progress feels elusive.

This process of slow, relentless change has been a central feature of every significant social movement in history. If we look at the civil rights movement in the United States, for example, it is clear that the victories of the 1960s, while monumental, were just one chapter in a much longer struggle. The movement for racial justice did not begin with Martin Luther King Jr. or Rosa Parks, nor did it end with the passage of the Civil Rights Act of 1964 or the Voting Rights Act of 1965. It was a struggle that had been ongoing for centuries, one that saw many moments of progress but also many setbacks and failures. Even after legal victories, the fight for racial equality continued through decades of resistance, protest, and organizing. The same is true for the feminist movement. The fight for women's suffrage was won with the passage of the 19th Amendment in 1920, but the battle for gender equality in all aspects of life, from the workplace to the home, from reproductive rights to political representation, has continued for over a century. These movements have made progress, but that progress has often come slowly, and it has come only after years of struggle, of persistence, and of never accepting that change is impossible.

The suffragists and suffragettes who fought for women's right to vote in the early 20th century faced ridicule, imprisonment, and violence. They were derided as "unladylike," "radical," and "unnatural" because they dared to challenge the status quo. Yet, despite these immense obstacles, they persisted. They organized, they protested, they lobbied, and they never gave up. They knew that the fight for women's rights was not a fight that could be won with one victory, one court case, or one march. It was a fight that required sustained action over generations. And while they achieved the right to vote, they knew that this was just the beginning, not the end, of their struggle.

In the face of systemic injustice, patience is not just a virtue, it is a necessary weapon. We cannot afford to lose sight of the long-term goals in the pursuit of short-term victories. That does not mean we should stop fighting for immediate change or push for reforms that will have an immediate impact. But we must always remember that these are steps along the way, not the destination. Whether we are fighting for reproductive rights, racial justice, climate action, or economic equity, the work we are doing today is part of a much larger, much longer struggle. The victories we win today, while important, are only part of the broader battle for a more just, equitable world.

Persistence is the thread that connects all successful movements. The women's rights movement, the civil rights movement, the labor movement, the LGBTQ+ rights movement, each of these movements achieved significant victories, but those victories did not come easily. They were the result of years, sometimes decades, of organizing, advocacy, and relentless struggle. The fight for gender equality, for example, is ongoing. Even in countries where women have gained the right to vote, access to education, and the ability to participate in the workforce, gender-based violence and inequality remain widespread. The fight for reproductive rights, for equal pay, for political representation, and for control over one's own body is far from over. In fact, in some places, women's rights are being rolled back, and the forces of patriarchy are pushing harder than ever to reclaim the ground they've lost.

One of the greatest challenges in these long, persistent struggles is the feeling of burnout. Change takes time, and in the face of setbacks, it can be easy to lose hope. The slow pace of progress can be demoralizing, and it's natural to feel frustrated when victories seem few and far between. But it is in these moments of frustration and fatigue that persistence becomes all the more important. When we feel as though we are not making any progress, it is essential to remember that every action we take is part of a larger effort, one that is moving us closer to our ultimate goal. The people who fought for women's suffrage didn't see the victory in their lifetime; neither did the civil rights activists of the 1960s. But their efforts laid the groundwork for the successes that would come later.

The resilience required to keep pushing forward is what ultimately wins in the long run. It is what sustains movements over generations and makes them capable of weathering the inevitable storms. History is full of examples of movements that, against all odds, ultimately succeeded because they never gave up. From the anti-apartheid movement in South Africa to the feminist movements that have changed the face of the world, the lesson is clear: persistence, more than any other quality, is what turns the tide. It is what transforms incremental change into revolutionary change. It is what ensures that the victories of today lead to the victories of tomorrow.

In the end, the slow grind of change may be frustrating, but it is also empowering. It is a reminder that the power to change the world does not reside with a single person or a single event. It resides with the collective efforts of countless individuals who, over time, build a movement strong enough to bring about lasting transformation. And when that transformation comes, when we look back at the long road we have traveled, we will see that every step, no matter how small it seemed at the time, was worth it. The persistence of individuals and movements, across generations, is what will ultimately bring about the revolution we seek. The long road ahead is not easy, but it is the only road worth traveling, because in the end, it is the persistence of those who refuse to give up that will change the world.

A Multi-Generational Plan For Actual Progress

The urgency for multi-generational change is critical, especially as the climate crisis accelerates. The 4B Movement—Burn, Ban, Boycott, Build—offers a blueprint for restructuring society into a compassionate, communal system, but the intensity of climate change events demands an adaptable, urgent response. As natural disasters, extreme weather, and environmental degradation increase, they will disrupt our plans, forcing faster adaptations. This multi-generational transformation must focus on not just survival, but the creation of resilient, sustainable communities led by women, who have historically been the backbone of care and community-building.

1. Rebuilding Communities (Next 5-10 Years)

In the face of climate disruptions, local, self-sustaining communities will be essential. These communities must become cooperative hubs, with women leading the charge. The focus should be on establishing mutual aid networks, local food systems, and disaster preparedness. This phase also involves restructuring education systems to emphasize cooperation, environmental stewardship, and empathy, ensuring future generations are ready to face a changed world. As climate events worsen, these communities will be the first line of defense and must be resilient and adaptable to rapidly changing circumstances.

2. Economic Transformation (Next 10-20 Years)

The current profit-driven, exploitative economy will collapse under the weight of climate change. As supply chains falter, cooperative, community-based economies will take precedence. Women should spearhead the creation of cooperative businesses, time banks, and sustainable economic models that prioritize care and community resilience. Public investments must shift to green infrastructure, renewable energy, and sustainable agriculture to withstand climate-related disruptions. This economic shift will ensure that communities can meet their needs even as global systems break down.

3. Decentralized Governance (Next 20-30 Years)

Governance must shift from centralized, hierarchical structures to decentralized, community-based systems that are more responsive to local needs, particularly in times of crisis. Women's leadership will be vital in shaping governance that focuses on climate justice, social welfare, and environmental sustainability. Direct democratic models where communities have a say in decision-making will replace traditional systems, enabling faster responses to local needs while ensuring equitable distribution of resources.

4. Global Solidarity and Climate Adaptation (Beyond 30 Years)

Global cooperation will be essential as the effects of climate change cross borders. International policies must prioritize climate justice, with women in leadership roles driving global efforts for fair resource distribution, climate reparations, and sustainable development. Through solidarity, communities worldwide can support one another, ensuring that vulnerable populations are not left behind.

As climate change continues to escalate, plans will need to evolve rapidly. More detailed strategies will be developed in response to each crisis, but the core principles—cooperation, sustainability, and justice—will guide the transformation. With women at the helm, we can build a world that not only survives but thrives, despite the challenges ahead.

Epilogue:
The City of the Chosen Few

In a near-future world where the balance of power had shifted, the women of Avalon Heights, a thriving metropolis at the heart of a global feminist revolution, decided they had waited long enough for men to fix the damage they had wrought. The old strategies of dialogue, compromise, and incremental progress had failed to reverse the tides of misogyny, environmental destruction, and systemic oppression. So, the women took a radical step. They declared that intimacy, long weaponized against them, would now be a privilege. Only men who actively fought to dismantle oppressive policies, combat climate change, and promote gender equality would be allowed the honor of physical and emotional connection. The rest were cast into the "Grey Zone," a bleak area of the city where men lived in isolation until they proved themselves worthy of rejoining society.

The rules of Avalon Heights were simple but transformative. For centuries, women had been expected to provide emotional labor, sexual fulfillment, and support to men regardless of how they were treated in return. Now, those dynamics had flipped. In Avalon Heights, men had to earn their place. The most committed and virtuous among them, the Chosen Few, were admitted into lush enclaves called Oases, where they lived among the women they served and supported. These districts were utopian havens filled with vibrant art, music, and life. Every wall was adorned with creations by women artists, every public space designed to prioritize women's comfort and safety. Here, relationships flourished under new terms: women led, and men followed.

Marcus, one of the first men granted access to the Oases, had earned his place through years of tireless work. As a climate scientist and activist, he had dedicated his life to reversing environmental destruction and dismantling the patriarchal policies that perpetuated it. He'd faced ridicule and resistance but persisted, knowing the stakes were too high to remain silent. When he crossed the threshold into Avalon Heights, he felt something shift. No longer was he the leader or the savior. Instead, he saw himself as a collaborator, working alongside women who were transforming society for the better. In the Oases, intimacy was not transactional but mutual, an act of joy shared between equals. Marcus often marveled at the life he lived now, saying, "I'm not here to fix things for women, I'm here to help them fix the mess we men made."

Outside the Oases, however, the Grey Zone told a different story. Men like John, who had spent their lives defending the status quo, found themselves exiled to the fringes of Avalon Heights. The Grey Zone was stark, a place where complacency and entitlement had no outlet. John's days blurred together as he sat in his cramped apartment, scrolling through online forums where other Grey Zone men vented their frustrations. "They've weaponized sex!" some shouted. "This isn't equality, it's tyranny!" Yet, even as they raged, they couldn't ignore the undeniable truth: Avalon Heights was thriving. Its women weren't lonely or miserable; they were thriving, joyful, and in complete control of their destinies.

For John, the Grey Zone was a wake-up call. He had mocked feminism, voted for politicians who gutted women's rights, and dismissed climate change as a hoax. But now, staring out at the glittering lights of the Oases, he began to wonder if he had been wrong all along. The men in Avalon Heights were not just granted access because they "played nice." They had transformed themselves, their actions, and their priorities. They fought for justice not out of guilt but because they saw the intrinsic value of equity and accountability. Slowly, John started to change. He joined community clean-ups, educated himself about feminist theory, and supported progressive candidates. Over time, he began to shed the layers of entitlement and defensiveness that had defined him for so long.

When John was finally invited to Avalon Heights, it wasn't just the physical space that felt different, it was his own sense of purpose. For the first time, he understood that equality wasn't a concession to women; it was a moral imperative that lifted everyone. Entering the Oasis, he realized that this wasn't about sex or privilege. It was about becoming part of a world where respect, collaboration, and mutual care replaced the hierarchy and dominance he had once accepted as natural.

As the movement spread beyond Avalon Heights, it rippled across cities and towns worldwide. Women took note of what was happening and began organizing their own revolutions. The Chosen Few of Avalon Heights became ambassadors, traveling to share their stories and help other men understand what true accountability looked like. Meanwhile, the men in the Grey Zones of the world faced a choice: cling to their resentment or embrace change.

The legacy of Avalon Heights was clear. Women had not only reclaimed their autonomy but also redefined the terms of intimacy and partnership. Sex was no longer a weapon or a gift. It was an act of connection, shared with those who truly valued it. The misogynists who once mocked this new order? Many remained in the Grey Zones, but those who evolved found a place in a better world. In the end, Avalon Heights wasn't just a city, it was a blueprint for a future where power was shared, the planet was healed, and women no longer had to wait for men to fix what they had broken.

For Further Community

1.   National Organization for Women (NOW): A grassroots organization promoting feminist ideals and working to eliminate discrimination. (Now.org)

2.   UN Women: The global champion for gender equality, working to develop and uphold standards and create an environment in which women and girls can thrive. (UN Women)

3.   Global Fund for Women: A feminist fund supporting grassroots movements for gender justice worldwide. (Global Fund for Women)

4.   Association for Women's Rights in Development (AWID): An international feminist membership organization committed to achieving gender equality, sustainable development, and women's human rights.

5.   MADRE: An international women's human rights organization that works to eliminate violence targeting women, girls, and LGBTQIA+ people of all genders. (Madre)

6.   Global Rights for Women: A nonprofit organization working to end gender-based violence against women and girls. (Global Rights for Women)

7.   Together Women Rise: A community of women and allies dedicated to achieving global gender equality. (Together Women Rise)

8.   Women's Refugee Commission: An organization focused on improving the lives and protecting the rights of women, children, and youth displaced by conflict and crisis.

9.   Women's International League for Peace and Freedom (WILPF): The oldest women's peace organization, working to achieve disarmament, human rights, and social justice.

10.   Women's World Banking: An organization empowering low-income women around the world through financial inclusion.

11.   World Association of Girl Guides and Girl Scouts: A global movement empowering girls and young women to develop their fullest potential.

12.   Young Women's Christian Association (YWCA): An organization dedicated to eliminating racism, empowering women, and promoting peace, justice, freedom, and dignity for all.

13.   Zonta International: A global organization of executives and professionals working together to advance the status of women worldwide through service and advocacy.

14.	AWID: An international feminist membership organization committed to achieving gender equality, sustainable development, and women's human rights.

15.	Association for Women's Rights in Development (AWID): An international feminist membership organization committed to achieving gender equality, sustainable development, and women's human rights.

16.	Women's Environment & Development Organization (WEDO): An organization advocating for women's equality in global policy.

17.	Women's International Democratic Federation (WIDF): An organization aimed at improving women's economic rights.

18.	Women's International Zionist Organization (WIZO): An organization providing community services in Israel and throughout the Jewish world.

19.	Women's World Banking: An organization empowering low-income women around the world through financial inclusion.

20.	Women's WorldWide Web (W4): An organization empowering women and girls around the world.

21.	World Pulse: A women's social network connecting women globally.

22.	Women Without Borders: An organization empowering women as agents of change.

23.	Women for Women International: An organization supporting women survivors of war.

24.	Women in Animation: An organization supporting women animators.

25.	Women in Parliaments Global Forum: An organization supporting women parliamentarians.

26.	Women in the World Foundation: An organization supporting women globally.

27.	Women's Commission for Refugee Women and Children: An organization defending the rights of refugee women, youth, and children.

28.	Women's International League for Peace and Freedom (WILPF): An organization working for women's peace.

29.	Women's International Democratic Federation (WIDF): An organization aimed at improving women's economic rights.

30.	Women's International Zionist Organization (WIZO): An organization providing community services in Israel and throughout the Jewish world.

Make Art and Love (not with men until they seriously get their shit together), Not War

Playlist for a Feminist Revolution

19th Century & Early 20th Century
Bread and Roses – Traditional labor song
No More Auction Block for Me – Traditional abolitionist song
The Women's Marseillaise – Suffragette anthem
Keep the Home Fires Burning – Ivor Novello
Solidarity Forever – Ralph Chaplin

1940s–1950s
Ain't Gonna Let Nobody Turn Me Around – Traditional civil rights song
Which Side Are You On? – Florence Reece
Strange Fruit – Billie Holiday
Move On Up a Little Higher – Mahalia Jackson
We Shall Overcome – Pete Seeger

1960s
Mississippi Goddam – Nina Simone
Respect – Aretha Franklin
Both Sides Now – Joni Mitchell
To Be Young, Gifted, and Black – Lorraine Hansberry (Donny Hathaway)
Blowin' in the Wind – Joan Baez

1970s
I Am Woman – Helen Reddy
Gloria – Patti Smith
The Pill – Loretta Lynn
What's Going On – Marvin Gaye
American Woman – The Guess Who

1980s
Bad Reputation – Joan Jett
Sisters Are Doin' It for Themselves – Eurythmics (feat. Aretha Franklin)
Love Is a Battlefield – Pat Benatar
Sweet Dreams (Are Made of This) – Annie Lennox
Fast Car – Tracy Chapman

1990s
Rebel Girl – Bikini Kill
Just a Girl – No Doubt
Zombie – The Cranberries
You Oughta Know – Alanis Morissette
Unpretty – TLC

2000s
Rock the Boat – Aaliyah
Family Affair – Mary J. Blige
Stupid Girls – Pink
Not Ready to Make Nice – Dixie Chicks
He Wasn't Man Enough – Toni Braxton

2010s
Run the World (Girls) – Beyoncé
The Man – Taylor Swift
Salute– Little Mix
Truth Hurts – Lizzo
Born This Way – Lady Gaga

Global Anthems
Malaika – Miriam Makeba
Gracias a la Vida – Violeta Parra
Quédate Callada – Mercedes Sosa
Fight Like a Girl – Zolita
Tīmatanga – Maisey Rika

Classic Protest Songs
Masters of War – Bob Dylan
Imagine – John Lennon
Get Up, Stand Up – Bob Marley
Where Have All the Flowers Gone? – The Kingston Trio
A Change Is Gonna Come – Sam Cooke

Empowerment Anthems
I Will Survive – Gloria Gaynor
Independent Women, Pt. 1 – Destiny's Child
Girl on Fire – Alicia Keys
Q.U.E.E.N. – Janelle Monáe (feat. Erykah Badu)
Praying – Kesha

Alternative & Indie
Dog Days Are Over – Florence + The Machine
Violet – Hole
Goodbye Earl – The Chicks
Cannonball – The Breeders
Maps – Yeah Yeah Yeahs

Hip-Hop & R&B
Can't Hold Us Down – Christina Aguilera (feat. Lil' Kim)
Let Me Blow Ya Mind – Eve (feat. Gwen Stefani)
Ladies First – Queen Latifah (feat. Monie Love)
Do Wop (That Thing) – Lauryn Hill
Work It – Missy Elliott

Hispanic
La Vida es un Carnaval – Celia Cruz
Malamente – Rosalía
La Rebelión – Joe Arroyo
Mi Gente – J Balvin and Willy William
Sin Miedo (del Amor y Otros Demonios) – Kali Uchis

Rock
Cherry Bomb – The Runaways
Because the Night – Patti Smith
Barracuda – Heart
Piece of My Heart – Janis Joplin
Edge of Seventeen – Stevie Nicks

Punk
Anarchy in the UK – Sex Pistols
Rise Above – Black Flag
Career Opportunities – The Clash
Fast Cars – Buzzcocks
Holiday in Cambodia – Dead Kennedys

Country & Folk
Coal Miner's Daughter – Loretta Lynn
Jolene – Dolly Parton
Independence Day – Martina McBride
Sin Wagon – Dixie Chicks
Take Me Home, Country Roads – John Denver

2020s Empowerment Hits
WAP – Cardi B (feat. Megan Thee Stallion)
Mother's Daughter – Miley Cyrus
Anti-Hero – Taylor Swift
Levitating – Dua Lipa
My Future – Billie Eilish

LGBTQ+ Pride Anthems
I'm Coming Out – Diana Ross
Freedom – George Michael
True Colors – Cyndi Lauper
Dancing On My Own – Robyn
True Colors – Cyndi Lauper

Iconic Ballads & Power Songs
Wind Beneath My Wings – Bette Midler
Hero – Mariah Carey
My Heart Will Go On – Céline Dion
Defying Gravity – Idina Menzel
Rolling in the Deep – Adele

Uplifting Group Anthems
Let It Go – Idina Menzel
Firework – Katy Perry
Don't Stop Believing – Journey
Happy – Pharrell Williams
We Are Family – Sister Sledge

Revolutionary Classics
A Hard Rain's a-Gonna Fall – Bob Dylan
What's Going On – Marvin Gaye
People Have the Power – Patti Smith
We're Not Gonna Take It – Twisted Sister
For What It's Worth – Buffalo Springfield

Female Cinema to Spark the Spirit

20' –40's
The Passion of Joan of Arc (1928)
His Girl Friday (1940)
Rebecca (1940)
Mildred Pierce (1945)
Gilda (1946)

1950s–1960s
All About Eve (1950)
Roman Holiday (1953)
Gigi (1958)
Breakfast at Tiffany's (1961)
The Sound of Music (1965)

1970s
Klute (1971)
The Stepford Wives (1975)
Julia (1977)
Norma Rae (1979)
Alien (1979)

1980s
Nine to Five (1980)
Silkwood (1983)
Aliens (1986)
Fatal Attraction (1987)
Working Girl (1988)

1990s
Thelma & Louise (1991)
A League of Their Own (1992)
The Piano (1993)
Little Women (1994)
G.I. Jane (1997)

2000s
Erin Brockovich (2000)
Frida (2002)
Kill Bill: Vol. 1 & 2 (2003–2004)
North Country (2005)
The Devil Wears Prada (2006)

2010s
Mad Max: Fury Road (2015)
Hidden Figures (2016)
Wonder Woman (2017)
Lady Bird (2017)
Captain Marvel (2019)

2020s
Promising Young Woman (2020)
Everything Everywhere All At Once (2022)
Women Talking (2022)
The Woman King (2022)
Barbie (2023)

International Female Power Films
The Blue Angel (1930, Germany)
La Femme Nikita (1990, France)
Amélie (2001, France)
Persepolis (2007, France/Iran)
Portrait of a Lady on Fire (2019, France)

Animated Films with Strong Female Leads
Mulan (1998)
Spirited Away (2001, Japan)
Brave (2012)
Frozen (2013)
Moana (2016)

Female Visual Artists

Artemisia Gentileschi (1593–1656)

Judith Leyster (1609–1660)

Rosalba Carriera (1675–1757)

Angelica Kauffman (1741–1807)

Élisabeth Vigée Le Brun (1755–1842)

Mary Cassatt (1844–1926)

Berthe Morisot (1841–1895)

Camille Claudel (1864–1943)

Käthe Kollwitz (1867–1945)

Georgia O'Keeffe (1887–1986)

Sonia Delaunay (1885–1979)

Tamara de Lempicka (1898–1980)

Frida Kahlo (1907–1954)

Lee Krasner (1908–1984)

Dorothea Tanning (1910–2012)

Louise Bourgeois (1911–2010)

Elaine de Kooning (1918–1989)

Helen Frankenthaler (1928–2011)

Bridget Riley (b. 1931)

Yayoi Kusama (b. 1929)

Agnes Martin (1912–2004)

Niki de Saint Phalle (1930–2002)

Eva Hesse (1936–1970)

Lygia Pape (1927–2004)

Judy Chicago (b. 1939)

Miriam Schapiro (1923–2015)

Faith Ringgold (b. 1930)

Ana Mendieta (1948–1985)

Shirin Neshat (b. 1957)

Kara Walker (b. 1969)

Cindy Sherman (b. 1954)

Barbara Kruger (b. 1945)

Jenny Holzer (b. 1950)

Rachel Whiteread (b. 1963)

Marina Abramović (b. 1946)

Carrie Mae Weems (b. 1953)

Tracey Emin (b. 1963)

Zanele Muholi (b. 1972)

Tania Bruguera (b. 1968)

Doris Salcedo (b. 1958)

Julie Mehretu (b. 1970)

Njideka Akunyili Crosby (b. 1983)

Cecily Brown (b. 1969)

Rachel Rose (b. 1986)

Toyin Ojih Odutola (b. 1985)

Mickalene Thomas (b. 1971)

Dana Schutz (b. 1976)

Haegue Yang (b. 1971)

Simone Leigh (b. 1967)

Firelei Báez (b. 1981)

Female Literature: Read, Absorb, & Put into Practice

The Tale of Genji by Murasaki Shikibu (11th century)
A Vindication of the Rights of Woman by Mary Wollstonecraft (1792)
Frankenstein by Mary Shelley (1818)
Jane Eyre by Charlotte Brontë (1847)
Wuthering Heights by Emily Brontë (1847)
Little Women by Louisa May Alcott (1868)
The Awakening by Kate Chopin (1899)
A Room of One's Own by Virginia Woolf (1929)
Their Eyes Were Watching God by Zora Neale Hurston (1937)
The Second Sex by Simone de Beauvoir (1949)
The Feminine Mystique by Betty Friedan (1963)
The Golden Notebook by Doris Lessing (1962)
To Kill a Mockingbird by Harper Lee (1960)
A Wrinkle in Time by Madeleine L'Engle (1962)
The Bell Jar by Sylvia Plath (1963)
The Left Hand of Darkness by Ursula K. Le Guin (1969)
I Know Why the Caged Bird Sings by Maya Angelou (1969)
Fear of Flying by Erica Jong (1973)
The Dispossessed by Ursula K. Le Guin (1974)
Woman on the Edge of Time by Marge Piercy (1976)
The Woman Warrior by Maxine Hong Kingston (1976)
Kindred by Octavia Butler (1979)
The Bloody Chamber by Angela Carter (1979)
Song of Solomon by Toni Morrison (1977)
Women, Race, & Class by Angela Davis (1981)
The Color Purple by Alice Walker (1982)
The Handmaid's Tale by Margaret Atwood (1985)
Beloved by Toni Morrison (1987)
Eva Luna by Isabel Allende (1987)
The Beauty Myth by Naomi Wolf (1990)
Possessing the Secret of Joy by Alice Walker (1992)
Women Who Run with the Wolves by Clarissa Pinkola Estés (1992)
The God of Small Things by Arundhati Roy (1997)
The Vagina Monologues by Eve Ensler (1998)
Persepolis by Marjane Satrapi (2000)
Braiding Sweetgrass by Robin Wall Kimmerer (2013)
We Should All Be Feminists by Chimamanda Ngozi Adichie (2014)
Bad Feminist by Roxane Gay (2014)
The Argonauts by Maggie Nelson (2015)

Shrill by Lindy West (2016)
The Power by Naomi Alderman (2016)
Hunger by Roxane Gay (2017)
Why I'm No Longer Talking to White People About Race by Reni
Eddo-Lodge (2017)
Witches, Sluts, Feminists by Kristen J. Sollee (2017)
Circe by Madeline Miller (2018)
Girl, Woman, Other by Bernardine Evaristo (2019)
Invisible Women: Data Bias in a World Designed for Men by
Caroline Criado Perez (2019)
Hood Feminism by Mikki Kendall (2020)

Female Forward TV

I Love Lucy (1951)
The Mary Tyler Moore Show
(1970)
Maude (1972)
Wonder Woman (1975)
Alice (1976)
Laverne & Shirley (1976)
Cagney & Lacey (1981)
Cheers (1982)
Designing Women (1986)
Roseanne (1988)
Murphy Brown (1988)
Clarissa Explains It All (1991)
Absolutely Fabulous (1992)
The Nanny (1993)
Xena: Warrior Princess (1995)
Buffy the Vampire Slayer
(1997)
Sex and the City (1998)
Gilmore Girls (2000)
Alias (2001)
The L Word (2004)
Veronica Mars (2004)
Grey's Anatomy (2005)
Ugly Betty (2006)
30 Rock (2006)
Parks and Recreation (2009)

The Good Wife (2009)
New Girl (2011)
Scandal (2012)
Orphan Black (2013)
Orange Is the New Black
(2013)
Broad City (2014)
Jane the Virgin (2014)
Crazy Ex-Girlfriend (2015)
The Marvelous Mrs. Maisel
(2017)
The Handmaid's Tale (2017)
Big Little Lies (2017)
Killing Eve (2018)
Pose (2018)
Dead to Me (2019)
Fleabag (2019)
Gentleman Jack (2019)
Mrs. America (2020)
I May Destroy You (2020)
The Queen's Gambit (2020)
WandaVision (2021)
Mare of Easttown (2021)
The Sex Lives of College Girls
(2021)
Yellowjackets (2021)
Abbott Elementary (2022)
A League of Their Own (2022)

Shhh…
Legend of Lysistrata or Legend of Post America

Shhh… The Legend of Lysistrata, or perhaps, the Legend of Post-America, begins in a time of unimaginable frustration, where the world had spun into chaos. The voices of women, long silenced by centuries of oppression, had finally found their echo. In the heart of this decaying world, Lysistrata, a woman of fierce resolve, stood as the symbol of resistance. Not just against war, but against the war waged on women's autonomy, their bodies, their voices. The world had forgotten its balance. Power was held by those who crushed it beneath their boots, men who took and took without ever asking if it was theirs to take. They had come to believe their grip on the world was unbreakable, their power absolute. But they underestimated the quiet force of women. Lysistrata, knowing that no battle could be fought with brute force alone, devised a plan, a plan so daring that no one thought it possible. She gathered women from every corner of the earth, calling them to action not with weapons, but with a refusal. A refusal to give what was so often taken without consent, love, sex, attention, care.

"Enough," Lysistrata said, her voice steady, fierce, and unwavering. "We will withhold what you need most. We will make you see, make you feel, what you've denied us all these years." And so they did. The women, united, withheld the one thing that had always kept them in the shadows, their power to give. Without it, men were left to crumble, lost and desperate. It wasn't cruelty. It wasn't punishment. It was a simple act of reclamation. The battlefields of the world fell silent. The systems that had long oppressed withered in the face of this quiet revolt. In the Legend of Post-America, the men were left to question their world, to question themselves, while the women, who had for so long been nothing more than vessels for male power, now stood as the architects of the future. The legend of Lysistrata lived on, a reminder that revolution starts with a single, resolute refusal.

List of Prints

About EATMS Productions

What's happening to women now is not random. It's structural.

Policy, culture, technology, and power are moving in the same direction.

EATMS maps them clearly and shows how to respond.

This title is part of an ongoing body of work. All EATMS Productions titles, across all series, authors, and formats, are components of a single connected project.

Start here: EATMS System Primer — Free Bundle
https://eatms.gumroad.com/l/dyvzbw

For full catalog or inquiries: eatms.me

Free survival booklet + EATMS updates: email "EATMS" to eatms@pm.me

Please feel free to burn part or all of this book, safely, as an effigy.